OVERCOME
SOCIAL ANXIETY

A Practical Guide to Symptoms, Causes, and Solutions. Discover How YOU Can Easily Cope with Panic Attacks, Phobias, and Depression and How to Improve YOUR Social Skills.

Dalton McKay

Table of Contents

Introduction.. ..1

Chapter 1: Social Anxiety, What Is It? Do You Recognize the Symptoms? 7

Physical and Psychological Symptoms .... .11

Social Anxiety and Depression.................................. .15

What Happens if You Think You Have Both? .... .28

Chapter 2: Causes of Social Anxiety........... 30

Genetic Causes 31

Psychological Causes 33

Personality..35

Environmental Factors 37

What is Serotonin?...50

Chapter 3: Phobias 53

What is a Phobia Disorder?..53

Types of Phobias 56

How Do Phobias Develop? 57

Common Phobias...60

Treatments of Phobias..64

Chapter 4: The Test 69

The Liebowitz Social Anxiety Scale Test.....................70

What Do the Range of Scores Mean?..........................73

Chapter 5: Self-Help Strategies to Cope With Social Anxiety.. 77

Social Coping...78

Emotional Coping 97

Chapter 6: Lifestyle Changes That May Help..113

Meditation/Relaxation Techniques 117

Help Other People...124

Find a Sense of Purpose...127

Consider Following a Spiritual Path 128

Chapter 7: How to Survive Real Life Situations
....**131**

Communication in the Workplace 132
Communication With Romantic Partners/Interests..135
Public Speaking..138

Chapter 8: Medical Treatments and Psychotherapy 141

Medical Treatments 141
Hypnosis..148
Cognitive Behavioral Therapy (CBT) 149
Other Types of Therapy 161
Alternative Treatments 165

Conclusion 169

Introduction

When you are thinking about the term 'anxiety' what do you immediately think of? Is it that wrenching feeling in your stomach? Or the inability to control the pace of your heart? Do you tend to hide away from people due to fear of social situations? Do you start thinking of all the worst possible outcomes of a certain situation?

Did you know that anxiety disorders are the most common mental illnesses in the United States presently? It currently affects 40 million adults, which is 18% of the entire population. That is not a small number. Historically, humans have experienced anxiety since the very beginning. Back in those days, anxiety was extremely helpful in order to protect us from dangerous situations.

Anxiety is a basic emotion and is an experience that literally all species of animals experience. It is what triggers the fight or flight response. However, in the modern-day, anxiety has become a much bigger problem, and instead of helping us survive and live, it is actually hindering many people's lives. Humans used to experience anxiety as a form of self-defense, but how would you explain social anxiety? People who experience social anxiety don't feel anxious because they are in the presence of danger; instead, they feel irrationally anxious at the thought of social situations.

Anxiety disorders only began to be recognized in the 1980s. Since then, we have come a long way in our research related to anxiety disorders. In the present day, we have solutions that range from behavioral therapy, talking therapies, meditation, and medication to help those who suffer from anxiety disorders.

Understanding your own level of social anxiety is important when it comes to finding the right treatment for you. Those who have severe levels of social anxiety may require medication, while those with moderate levels may only require therapy and a change in lifestyle.

By reading this book, you will be able to understand your own level of social anxiety more and figure out what treatments you feel like are best for you.

Keep in mind that if you suspect that you have a social anxiety disorder or any type of mental disorder in general, then you should seek help from a licensed health professional immediately. Mental health is a serious matter, and it is not possible to properly diagnose your specific illness by reading a book. Seeing a licensed professional can help properly diagnose you, and they can provide professional advice on treatment plans that are specific to you.

In the early chapters of this book, you will learn about what social anxiety is, its symptoms, and its relationship with depression. You will also get to study what the causes are so you can identify the likelihood of you having it. I will also touch upon phobia disorders and help you get familiarized with the different types, how it develops, and the causes and treatments of it.

Towards the middle chapters of this book, you will be taught a test that you can do to measure a person's social anxiety. This is a tool that a health professional may use to assess their patient's level of social anxiety to determine what type of treatment is best prescribed.

At the end of this book, you will learn about different strategies that can be used to help a person cope with social anxiety. You will also be taught the different aspects of lifestyle changes that one can make that has been proven to help improve social anxiety.

I will also provide you with practical advice on how you can utilize simple communication skills to help you get through anxiety-inducing real-life situations. Last but not least, you will familiarize with the different medical treatments and psychotherapy that can be utilized to help social anxiety. You will learn about the different types of medication and therapies, such as Cognitive Behavioral Therapy, that have a strong track record of helping those that suffer from depression and anxiety.

Identifying your personal level of social anxiety is crucial in the process of overcoming it. This is why seeing a health professional to get a proper diagnosis is an extreme priority. As you are reading through this book, pay extra attention to the causes and symptoms of social anxiety. If you are someone who is unsure about your anxiety levels at the moment, these are important topics to focus on.

Learning about the causes can help you understand your family background further and help you get an idea of your likelihood of being diagnosed with certain mental health disorders. Moreover, knowing the symptoms will help you take a more in-depth look at everything you're experiencing recently to help you determine whether or not you are showcasing some of these symptoms.

If you are in the early stages of recognizing some symptoms, it does not necessarily indicate that you have an anxiety disorder. Feeling anxious occasionally during social situations does NOT mean that you have social anxiety. Just like how someone who is feeling sadness during a time of grief doesn't mean that they have a depression disorder.

If you're ready for this journey, let's jump right in!

Chapter 1: Social Anxiety, What Is It? Do You Recognize the Symptoms?

Before we get into what social anxiety is, we first have to learn about anxiety as a general term. A lot of the time, when people use the term 'anxiety,' they are referring to generalized anxiety. Anxiety is a basic feeling and experience that literally all species of animals experience. Although anxiety is not a pleasant feeling, it is not dangerous.

Actually, anxiety is helpful for us in certain situations. Some people wish to get rid of anxiety completely, but that goal isn't possible or realistic! When it comes to Cognitive Behavioral Therapy, the approach is to help you build the skills required to help you manage and understand your anxiety as opposed to getting rid of it altogether (again, not possible).

We all have to keep in mind that anxiety is a normal emotion and that it is not dangerous. The symptoms of anxiety actually serve a function.

Anxiety is actually a natural reaction to a perceived threat and helps us humans respond to it. However, if you have excessive anxiety, it can also be a problem.

Since anxiety is a normal response to a threat, when a person perceives that they are in a threatening situation, their fight or flight instinct is triggered which its sole purpose is to protect itself by fighting or fleeing from danger. When somebody is feeling threatened, their brain sends messages to your autonomic nervous system (this is a section of your nerves). When this nervous system reacts, adrenalin and noradrenalin are released from your brain, which then triggers the anxiety response and automatically prepares us for danger. This nervous system is eventually stopped when these chemicals are destroyed by our bodies in an attempt to calm the body down.

This fact is extremely important to remember because those who suffer from anxiety disorders are convinced that their anxiety will go on forever. However, biologically this cannot happen since anxiety is limited by time. Although it may feel that the anxiety is going on forever, it has a limited lifespan. After some time, your body will determine that it has had enough with the fight or flight instinct and restore the body to its neutral feeling. Anxiety cannot continue endlessly or damage your body. Although highly uncomfortable, this whole cycle is perfectly harmless and natural. In fact, this behavior is instinctual to us because, in the wild, it is necessary for our bodies to be reactive to this response because we know that danger can return.

Overall, the fight or flight response activates the entire body's metabolism. This is what makes someone feel hot, flushed, and tired afterward because the entire process uses up a lot of energy. After a strong anxiety experience, most people feel drained, tired, and completely washed out.

What is an Anxiety Disorder?

Now that you know what anxiety is, and how it is a natural emotion that we feel for protection -

what is an anxiety disorder? An anxiety disorder is a medical condition where the individual feels symptoms of extreme anxiety or panic. In other words, an anxiety disorder is when the individual is feeling severe anxiety or panic and is unable to manage their symptoms. Let's take a look specifically into what a social anxiety disorder is.

What is Social Anxiety?

Although it is very normal to feel a certain level of nervousness in social situations, it is not normal to feel an overwhelming amount of anxiety. Situations such as attending formal events, public speaking, and doing presentations are likely events in which you feel some nervousness and anxiety. However, for those who suffer from social anxiety (or otherwise known as social phobia), speaking or performing in front of other people and general social situations can lead to extreme anxiety.

This usually stems from the fear of being criticized, judged, humiliated, or laughed at in front of other people. A lot of times, they are afraid of trivial and ordinary matters. For example, those who suffer from social anxiety may feel that eating at a restaurant around other people can be extremely daunting.

Social anxiety usually occurs during the lead up to performance events (e.g., having to give a speech or working while they are being watched) and situations where social interaction is involved (e.g., having lunch with coworkers or normal small talk). Social anxiety also occurs during the actual event, as well as the lead-up. Moreover, this type of phobia can also be very specific where the individual has a fear of a specific situation. For example, they can be fearful of having to be assertive during work meetings.

Physical and Psychological Symptoms

The symptoms of social anxiety include psychological and physical symptoms. People with social phobia find it very distressing when they experience physical symptoms. These physical symptoms include:

- Excessive perspiration

- Nausea/Diarrhea

- Trembling

- Stammering, stuttering, or blushing when speaking

When these physical symptoms occur, it normally causes the anxiety to increase as the person begins to fear that other people will notice these signs. However, these signs are usually not noticeable to other people. Those who suffer from this condition say that they also excessively worry that they will say or do something wrong, which will lead to a terrible result.

Often, people with social anxiety will attempt to avoid situations where they feel like there is a possibility for them to act in a way that is embarrassing or humiliating. If they can't avoid certain situations, they will choose to endure it but will become very distressed and anxious and may try to exit that situation as fast as they can. This can begin to have a negative effect on their relationships. Moreover, it may begin to affect their professional lives and their ability to maintain their daily routine.

A typical diagnosis of social anxiety is based on having the symptoms mentioned above and how much distress and impairment it causes on the individual's day to day routine. Usually, if symptoms continue for 6 months, then a diagnosis will be made.

Some social phobia symptoms that are psychological include:

- Feeling extreme nervousness before performing in front of other people

- Feeling extreme nervousness before meeting unfamiliar people

- Feeling embarrassment when being observed (e.g., eating or drinking in front of others, talking on the phone in front of others)

- Not going to certain events or interactions due to the fear of social nervousness

- Having difficulty going about daily life (e.g., studying, seeing friends, and working)

Based on research, it suggests that 11% of the population has experienced social anxiety in their lifetime. It showed that women experience this disorder more than men. Often, this phobia starts during childhood or adolescence.

So, what exactly causes social anxiety? There are numerous causes, but the most common ones are temperament, family history, and learned behavior. When it comes to temperament, children or adolescents who are shy are at more risk than others. Specifically, for children, those who exhibit shyness and timidity put them at risk of developing social anxiety in their adulthood. Family history is also a possibility when it comes to cause due to genetic predisposition. The main cause, however, is usually learned behavior. Those who suffer from social anxiety often developed this condition due to being treated poorly, embarrassed in public, or humiliated.

When it comes to treating social phobia, psychological treatments will be the first line of treatment, and in more severe cases, medication can be effective. Since social phobia is a type of anxiety disorder, many professionals choose to use Cognitive Behavioral Therapy as a treatment method. Later on in this book, we will be talking about how CBT helps treat anxiety disorders.

Social Anxiety and Depression

As I mentioned at the very beginning of this book, if you are diagnosed with one mental disorder, you are at a higher risk of developing others if your disorder is left untreated. A depressed person may not have experienced social anxiety at the beginning of their diagnosis, but if they leave their condition untreated, they may find themselves experiencing more social anxiety symptoms. This is the same vice versa as someone who is diagnosed with social anxiety may experience more depressive symptoms later on if it's left untreated. Let's take a deeper look into how many mental disorders are related, especially those that have to do with anxiety.

How are Different Mental Disorders Related?

As you have just learned, a lot of times, having one anxiety disorder can lead to a higher risk of developing other ones. Let's use Obsessive Compulsive Disorder as an example. An individual who is suffering from OCD often feels a lot of shame and secrecy when it comes to their compulsive tendencies.

Often, they don't want to showcase their tendencies around other people. This then creates a fear of being around other people. Having a fear of interacting and being around others is also a sign of a social disorder. If one anxiety disorder is left untreated for long periods of time, it is likely that those symptoms will snowball into other ones.

All anxiety disorders have one thing in common; worry. Since worry is the largest component of anxiety and is actually responsible for generating the emotion of anxiety, if someone is unable to manage their worry - they will likely become anxious and exhibit anxious behaviors. The worry that causes someone to develop Generalized Anxiety Disorder is the same worry that can cause someone to develop panic disorders. When someone is dealing with an overwhelming amount of worry, their environmental factors play a part in determining what type of disorder it manifests into.

For instance, let's use two Bob and John as examples. Bob and John both experience the same amount of worry. Bob grew up in an environment where his parents exhibited excessive cleaning behaviors. John grew up in an environment where he was timid and never learned how to break out of his shyness. Assuming the amount of worry that Bob and John are facing is equal, Bob is likely to develop an obsessive-compulsive disorder because of his exposure to his parents' cleaning tendencies. However, John is likely to develop social anxiety disorder due to his childhood and the lack of help to work through his timid personality.

The common factor in anxiety disorders is the worry, which then manifests into anxiety. Environmental factors affect what these anxieties become, which affects what their behavior will be. Like we discussed earlier, those who are suffering from one anxiety disorder may develop another one if the first isn't treated within a reasonable time frame.

Similarities and Differences between Social Anxiety and Depression

If you think you are someone who may be both depressed and suffering from social anxiety, studying the similarities and differences of its symptoms is extremely important. We know that social anxiety means an anxiety disorder that primarily gets triggered during social situations. This can be in the form of talking to other people, public speaking, or even as extreme as going out to places where there are other people. We also just learned about all its symptoms. However, what exactly is depression? In this subchapter, we will take a look at what depression actually means and the symptoms that come with it.

What is Depression?

Let's take a look at what depression actually is. The dictionary definition of depression is 'feelings of severe despondency and dejection.' However, we have to keep in mind to not get mix depression up with feelings of sadness or grief. The death of a loved one or the ending of a relationship are both very difficult experiences for a person to experience and endure. During these hard times, it is completely normal for feelings of sadness and grief to arise in response to those situations. People who are experiencing an event of a loss might often describe themselves as being 'depressed.'

With that said, being sad is not the same as having the disorder of depression. A person's grieving process is unique to every individual, but it does share a lot of the same feelings that a depression disorder brings. Both depression and feelings of grief involve the feelings of sadness and withdrawal from a person's usual activities. Here are a few important reasons as to why they are different:

- When a person is feeling emotions of grief, their painful feelings often come in waves. They are usually mixed with positive memories about the person who's passed. When a person is feeling intense grief, their interest and mood are decreased for around two weeks.
- When a person is in grief, their self-esteem usually does not change much. When a person has depression, they have constant feelings of self-loathing and worthlessness.
- For most people, the death of a loved one can cause major depression. For other people, it could be losing their job or being a victim of physical assault. When depression and grief are co-existing, grief is

usually a more severe feeling and lasts longer than grief without depression. There is some overlap between depression and grief, but despite this, they are still different. Helping a person distinguish between grief and depression is necessary in order to help them get help, support, or treatment.

Let's take a look at the symptoms of depression. By understanding which symptoms are caused by depression, it can help people identify the difference between a period of grieving to an actual depression disorder. When a person is feeling sad, having negative thoughts, or having trouble sleeping, it does not necessarily mean that they have depression. In order for a person to be diagnosed with a depression disorder, they must be exhibiting these traits:

- The person's symptoms must be new to them or be noticeably worse compared to how they were prior to the depressive episode.

- The person's symptoms must persist for most of the day and be as consistent as nearly every day for at least two consecutive weeks.
- The episode that this person experiences must also be accompanied by impaired functioning or clinically significant distress.

When you begin to suspect that you may have a depression disorder, it is extremely important to discuss all of the symptoms that you may be experiencing. The goal of depression treatments is to help people feel more like themselves again so that they are able to enjoy the things that they used to do. In order to achieve this, professionals must be able to find the right treatment in order to alleviate and address all their symptoms.

Even if a person is prescribed medication that is suitable for their type of depression, this may take quite a bit of time. In fact, some people are required to try different medications until they find one that works best for their specific body. The goal of depression treatment is not only focused on getting better, it's mainly focused on staying better.

We have to remember throughout this book that depression is not a simple change of mood or a moment of 'weakness.' Depression is a real medical condition that has many behavioral, physical, emotional, and cognitive symptoms. We will begin talking about all the different types of depression symptoms.

Emotional Symptoms

The most common symptoms of depression are emotional symptoms. These symptoms are the ones that affect your state of mind. Here are examples of a few emotional symptoms that people with depression have to endure:

- **Constant sadness:** This symptom is the feeling of sadness that occurs in a depressed person for no apparent reason. This feeling can feel very intense; it often feels like nothing can make it go away.

- **Feeling of worthlessness:** A person that is depressed often experiences unrealistic feelings of worthlessness or guilt. Usually, there isn't a specific event that provokes these feelings; they just happen at random.

- **Suicidal or dark thoughts:** These types of thoughts can occur very frequently during a person's depression. These thoughts have to be taken very seriously, and when a person is experiencing these emotions, they must ask for help right away.

- **Loss of interest or pleasure in activities that were previously enjoyed:** A person that is depressed may experience a loss of interest that affects all areas of their life. This can range from not finding pleasure from their previous hobbies to everyday activities that the person used to enjoy.

Physical Symptoms

Physical symptoms play a huge role in a person's depression. Usually, when people experience physical symptoms, they are close to discovering that they may have depression. Many people think that depression is limited to emotional symptoms, but this is untrue. Here are a few physical symptoms of depression:

- **Low energy:** People that have depression typically always feel like they are low on energy even if they have not exerted themselves. This type of depressive fatigue is different in the sense that neither sleep nor rest can alleviate this tiredness.

- **Psychomotor impairment:** Depression can make a person feel as if everything is slowed down. This includes slowed speech, body movement, thinking, speech that is in low volume, long pauses before answering, inflection, or muteness.

- **Aches and pains:** Depression can often cause physical pain. This includes joint pain, stomach pain, headaches, back pain, or other pains.

- **Insomnia or hypersomnia:** When a person is depressed, their sleep is often broken up and feels unrefreshing. As they wake up, they're usually in some type of mental anguish that prevents them from falling back to sleep. Other cases can be the opposite where the person is excessively sleeping.

- **Change in weight:** A change in a person's weight is a significant sign for professionals that are diagnosing depression.

Behavioral Symptoms

Besides emotional and physical symptoms, behavioral symptoms also play a huge role when it comes to diagnosing depression. Some behavioral symptoms include:

- **Change in appetite:** The most common of all behavioral symptoms of depression is a decrease in appetite. People with depression report that food seems tasteless, and they think all servings are too large. In addition, some people increase their food consumption instead, especially sweet foods, which can result in weight gain.

- **Impression of restlessness:** For some people, depression makes them very jumpy and agitated. They may struggle with sitting still, not pacing, fiddling with items, or hand-wringing.

Cognitive Symptoms

Cognitive symptoms are one of the least talked about symptoms when it comes to depression. This one is hard to diagnose, as many people don't know if they are experiencing it. The main cognitive symptom of depression is as follows:

- **Difficulty making decisions or focusing:** A person that is depressed may be caused to experience a lower ability to concentrate or think. This causes them to exhibit behaviors of indecisiveness.

What Happens if You Think You Have Both?

Now that you have seen the difference in symptoms of social anxiety compared to depression, you can see that there are quite a number of differences. However, there are a handful of similarities, such as a change in appetite and sleep pattern. If you are someone who thinks you are depressed and have social anxiety, then these two illnesses may actually be feeding off each other.

Depression may be causing you to lose interest in things that you used to love, like socializing. If you are someone who used to enjoy spending time with friends and family and you now have zero interest in it – this may be caused by depression. The longer you spend not socializing and communicating with other people, the more this unhealthy behavior may be feeding into your social anxiety.

Vice versa, if you are someone who used to enjoy socializing but now you are too anxious to be around other people, you may be causing depressive symptoms due to you being unable to do something you once loved. When someone is diagnosed with two different disorders, it's really hard to say which one is feeding into which. The only way around it is to start treating both disorders in order to reduce the overall amount of symptoms.

The first thing to do in a situation like this is getting an assessment of how severe each of your disorders are. If you are looking into your depression, do you think you have mild, moderate, or severe depression? If you are looking into your anxiety, do you think you have both GAD and social anxiety? If so, how severe are your symptoms? Once you get an idea of the severity of both disorders, you can start selecting treatment plans that can begin to treat both of those disorders. Cognitive Behavioral Therapy is a good example of a treatment that has effectively treated people with multiple mental disorders.

Chapter 2: Causes of Social Anxiety

As we learned while discussing different types of anxiety disorders, there are many external factors that can contribute to anxiety. The main factors that cause anxiety include:

- Genetic Causes: Family history.

- Psychological Causes: Childhood upbringing.

- Personality/temperament.

These are all factors that we are unable to control but plays a huge part in whether someone develops an anxiety disorder or not. Let's dive into these factors deeper.

Genetic Causes

Unlike physical traits like eye color, hair color, or facial features, anxiety in the family isn't easily identifiable through its generations. The search for the specific genes that are related to social anxiety disorder is still in the works. Researchers recently analyzed the genetic makeup of over 1000 different families, some of which suffered from social anxiety. They found that the gene they were researching was not associated with social anxiety.

However, a few years later, they drew another conclusion based on different research that led them to believe that there may be a link between the occurrence of social anxiety and our DNA code. These ideas need to be further studied, but as of right now, professionals believe that there is a relationship.

Psychologists predict that individuals can inherit a genetic predisposition to being an anxious person. Genetic predisposition to anxiety likely starts young. Studies show that when someone develops anxiety before the age of 20, close relatives are more likely to have anxiety as well.

Researchers have tried to study the genetics behind anxiety disorders just by looking at whether or not relatives have the same ones.

They discovered that people who are at a greater risk of anxiety disorders have a twin who also has the disorder. The likelihood of having an anxiety disorder is highest when it is a first-degree relative like a sibling or parent. Although studies show that the risk of anxiety does run in families, the role of its genetic influence compared with the family environment still remains unclear.

Psychological Causes

Often times, the way that a child was raised plays a significant role in how the child's emotional health is shaped. One of the key factors that influence anxiety disorders later on in life is overprotection from the parents. Overinvolved and overprotective parenting have been proven to reduce opportunities for the child to learn and experience. Since these opportunities have been reduced, professionals theorize that the child is less likely to be able to perceive a threat, learn to accurately detect a threat, and have difficulty coping with difficult situations.

Another type of parenting style called 'critical parenting' has been linked to developing emotional health problems in the child. This type of parenting has also been linked to the development of depression and anxiety in the later life of the child. The theory behind this is that if a parent criticizes and minimizes a child's feelings, this actually sabotages the child's ability to regulate emotion and increases their sensitivity to mental health problems such as depression and anxiety.

If parents often showcase fearful and avoidant behaviors, it is more likely to increase the child's risk of developing an anxiety disorder. A parent who is anxious or even suffering from an anxiety disorder is more likely to showcase this behavior, which then influences the child's behavior and, eventually, increasing the risk of the child developing an anxiety disorder. In addition, parents and children who have an insecure attachment are at a higher risk of developing anxiety disorders.

Since attachment is defined as the deep emotional bond between a child and parent, an insecure attachment may lead to many future problems. It is theorized that an insecure attachment occurs when the parent is insensitive and unresponsive to the child's needs. This insecure attachment has been associated with the development of anxiety disorders and depression during adulthood. Children that have experienced this insecure attachment are not capable of developing the emotion regulation skills needed to manage anxiety or positive self-esteem.

Personality

One of the major relationships within the world of anxiety is the relationship between personality and anxiety. Some even argue that anxiety can be thought of as a personality trait. For instance, if someone was taught growing up that being anxious helps produce successful outcomes or is the default feeling to most scenarios, anxiety can become a part of this person's personality when dealing with relationships, work, and the future.

When children are young, some will avoid social encounters and withdraw when in unfamiliar social settings, which leads to them being less assertive and more subjected to rejection from their peers. This also then leads to a negative self-perception. Due to this, children who are born with quieter and shyer temperaments often have fewer friends, which leads to increased anxiety and loneliness.

Research regarding the risk of anxiety focuses on the early temperaments of children, particularly those who are more inhibited. They found that around 60% of 13-year-olds that were inhibited at two years old showed very obvious signs of anxiety during social interactions. They compared this to other 13-year-olds that didn't show signs of inhibition at two years of age, and only 27% of this group showed signs of anxiety during social interactions. Further research showed that kids that are inhibited from the ages of 1 and 7 increased their odds by four times of being diagnosed with an anxiety disorder in adulthood.

Environmental Factors

Environmental factors are one of the most dominant causes of an individual having an increase in anxiety or developing a social anxiety disorder. Stress from work, school, relationships, and financial stress all contribute largely to anxiety disorders. Often times, somebody who hasn't suffered from an anxiety disorder before may develop one due to too much stress.

In this subchapter, we will be exploring the numerous environmental causes of social anxiety. We will dive into the different causes and some examples of each.

Stress at Work/School

Stress from work and/or school is one of the biggest contributing factors to social anxiety in the modern-day. Millions of people begin therapy to help control the anxiety and stress that they feel from work. In the present day, our society has fostered a toxic work culture where overworking yourself and being overly stressed is an indication that you are a good employee.

This has created a terrible mindset for many people, especially those who are in fields like sales, technology, and real estate. With this type of mindset in place, people are struggling to find balance in their lives to take care of themselves and are constantly anxious regarding what others would think of them if they weren't working themselves to death.

Here's an example to explain further how toxic work culture causes stress which then leads to social anxiety.

Jennifer is a salesperson in the field of technology. The company she works in fosters a competitive culture and values hard work and discipline. Everybody that works there has a type A personality and has a strong need to prove themselves and outwork other people. Jennifer has hit all her sales targets so far this year, and her boss is celebrating her hard work in front of the whole office.

However, she feels even though she is doing good, she is anxious that with this public attention, she may fail in front of the whole office if she does not continue to hit every target this year. This has caused her to feel extremely anxious when coming to work, and often, she finds herself sick with worry, although her track record is excellent.

Do you see how in this example that Jennifer is doing very well at work but yet she is sick with worry? With a toxic work culture where nothing is ever good enough, and you need to continue striving for more, this prevents people from feeling satisfied. By not feeling satisfied, most people will strive to hit goals to achieve that feeling, but they never do. This type of work culture is proven by many studies to create anxiety disorders in people that may have never had it before.

Stress From Relationships

Stress from relationships is also a very common cause for anxiety and, more specifically, social anxiety. This particularly affects people that have suffered from bad relationships in the past. The stress typically comes from one person being afraid that their partner is mad at them or going to leave them. This develops a constant worry of thoughts like 'Did I do something wrong?' or 'Is someone so going to break up with me?'. These thoughts continue to spiral until they are catastrophizing and eventually creates not only anxiety about the relationship but general anxiety as well.

Here is an example to explain how stress from relationships can contribute to a person's anxiety. Jennifer is in a long-distance relationship with her partner. Her partner has not been as responsive lately, and they don't have any plans to visit each other anytime soon. Due to her past experience of relationships not working out, she is afraid that her partner is either mad at her, or wants to break up with her by creating some distance. She begins to be consumed by these thoughts and finds it hard to focus at work, which makes her stressed about her work performance. She finds that she is just thinking about her relationship all day and is having difficulty concentrating on anything else.

We used Jennifer again in this example to show how stress from a relationship can cause anxiety. In this example, you can see that Jennifer begins to stress about she thinks her relationship won't work out, and it begins to dominate her mind and take concentration away from other parts of her life. The constant stress of thinking about her relationship and all the things that can go wrong begin to take over other aspects of her life, which creates anxiety as she is unable to cope with all of it. Extreme stress from one part of your life can begin to affect you in general, which then seeps into other aspects of your life (in this example, Jennifer begins to lose concentration at work which creates anxiety in that area as well).

Financial Stress

One of the reasons why people in the lower class income tend to report more anxiety disorders is due to financial stress. The stress of trying to make little money spread as thin as possible is something that can easily dominate a person's thoughts. Moreover, a sudden change in somebody's financial health can be a big contributor to stress. If someone is used to a certain style of living, if it dramatically changes for the worse, it may cause stress because this person is desperately trying to restore things to how they used to be, and will cause anxiety if this person is unsuccessful at it.

Here is an example of how financial stress can affect an individual. Jennifer has had a very successful sales career at the company she's been working at. She had recently saved enough money to purchase her first house. Since getting the mortgage, her monthly expenses have skyrocketed, and she has much less spending money than she used to. She began to have to stress over little things like, buying the cheapest groceries or downgrading her cell phone/internet plan to save money.

Since she was used to the comfort of having a lot of expendable income, it is bringing her stress to have to carefully watch her money every time she spends. She finds herself consumed by this stress and is anxious every time she is in a situation where money is involved.

In this example, we discussed how Jennifer went from having lots of expendable income to make her life more comfortable having much less. This can cause stress on you because now you have to make less money to work in all the places you needed to before. Although this example is not as severe compared to other examples of those who struggle to make rent and put food on the table, simple financial stress is enough to cause anxiety if it's not properly dealt with.

Emotional Trauma

Past or present emotional trauma can be a huge contributor to stress. This can be in the form of a breakup, death of someone you know, or experiencing a traumatic experience. Often times, when something traumatic happens to us, our brains are not equipped to process it properly. Instead, our defense mechanisms kick in and work hard to try to block the trauma out.

Most of the time, this is not a successful tactic, and we end up in this vicious cycle of trying to block it out but becoming frustrated when we are unsuccessful.

This is why it is extremely important to go and seek help when you have experienced something traumatic as trying to repress these thoughts causes stress, which then leads to general anxiety.

Here is an example of how emotional trauma can cause stress and anxiety in an individual. One of Jennifer's best friends had recently passed away due to a car accident. She doesn't know how to process this as nobody close to her has ever passed away before. She is overcome with grief but does not know how to cope with it and is simply just trying not to think about it.

When she catches herself thinking about her friend's death, she begins to sob uncontrollably and tries to force herself to push it away from her mind. She gets increasingly more stressed as she becomes more afraid of not being able to control this grief properly, she may have an uncontrollable cry at work or in other public places. She begins to feel anxious that people can tell she is about to cry and begins to worry that others around her will also get into a fatal accident.

In this example, you can see that the anxiety that Jennifer is feeling comes from two places. The first place is that she is afraid that she cannot contain her grief properly, and people will judge her for crying in a professional environment. The second place is that she is afraid that fatal accidents will happen to other people she loves. By not facing the grief and analyzing her feelings, she begins to be even more confused and spends most of her energy trying to push those thoughts away. Emotional trauma typically needs to be acknowledged and talked about within the first few days of the event as the longer it manifests in someone, the harder it is to analyze later.

Side Effects From Medication

Medications can cause different side effects in different people. Medications can cause stress if the drugs are made to target the same parts of your body that manages anxiety symptoms. Drugs that can cause anxiety as a side effect include; medications with caffeine, corticosteroids, ADHD drugs, and asthma medication. Many headache and migraine medicines are made with caffeine. Caffeine stimulates your nervous system, which increases your heart rate and blood pressure which will lead to jittery, nervous, and anxious feelings.

If you are someone who is prone to anxiety, caffeine is a big culprit in heightening those symptoms. Corticosteroids are a drug that works to mimic the hormones that your body makes. They are used to treat conditions such as allergies, arthritis, asthma and bronchitis. There isn't a lot of research presently about why these drugs make people irritable and anxious. ADHD drugs are mainly stimulants that are used to rev up your brain. These drugs are used to change the way your nervous systems send messages. It often can make you feel restless and anxious, especially if you are medicating on high doses.

Lastly, asthma medication has been proven to make mental disorders worse such as anxiety and depression. The drugs that are used to treat asthma are known for causing trembling or shaking, sweating, nervousness, and racing heartbeats. These are all symptoms of anxiety, and these drugs can heighten those symptoms significantly.

Stress From Medical Illness

Having a serious medical illness can cause a lot of stress for an individual. As mentioned above, if this medical illness requires medicine that contributes to anxiety, it may be the reason behind increased anxiety. However, if you have a medical illness that hinders your ability to live your daily life, it begins to cause stress in those areas aside from the stress of worrying about this medical illness. This is why often times when someone has a serious medical condition, their doctor would advise them to seek out support from family or friends or other support groups. This is crucial to learn how to manage the stress that comes with having a medical illness;

otherwise, the stress on the body may actually make that condition worse.

Stress From Drug Use

There is a constant debate between researchers in the psychology field regarding which comes first: drug use or anxiety? It could work both ways where the usage of drugs causes anxiety or having an anxiety disorder causes usage of drugs. Having both of these leads to a vicious cycle that tends to make both disorders worse. Often times if a person is suffering from anxiety in other parts of their life, they may turn to drug-use to alleviate some of that stress.

However, those who use drugs in general, despite having anxiety or not, may develop an anxiety disorder due to the effects of the drugs or withdrawal. They can also experience anxiety due to the financial stress of having to continuously purchase drugs to prevent withdrawal. If you find that you may be suffering from a substance use disorder, please seek help from your family doctor right away. When treated early, the effects of this disorder will be substantially decreased.

Low Self-Esteem

Low self-esteem is another major cause of social anxiety. Having low self-esteem is more complex than just a negative feeling. Low self-esteem takes a huge toll on people's lives. Although it is difficult to determine how common low self-esteem is, many scientific studies have found evidence that self-esteem levels drop significantly for people that are approaching their teenagehood. People in this age group often begin believing that they aren't 'good enough' in many aspects like relationships, physical appearance, and school performance.

When low self-esteem starts at a young age for people, it has a higher chance of being carried into adulthood. This is where it begins to interfere with the importance of things like a person's ability to live a fulfilling and healthy life. Oftentimes, low self-esteem transforms into mental disorders such as depression and anxiety.

An important aspect of self-esteem is that it is not an accurate reflection of reality, nor is it something that is set in stone. The cause of self-esteem can sometimes be found, but the belief that your feelings about yourself cannot be changed is an inaccurate one.

If you are interested in improving your self-esteem, I wrote a book on the subject that you can find on Amazon. Go to the last page of this book and you will find the direct link.

What is Serotonin?

Serotonin is a type of neurotransmitter that has been heavily linked to mental health. Low levels of serotonin have been found to be related to depression, general anxiety, and social anxiety. In its simplest form, the chemical 'messengers' in our brain are called neurotransmitters. The nerve cells within our brain use these messengers, aka neurotransmitters to communicate with one another. We believe that the messages that they send play a huge role in a person's mood regulation. The three neurotransmitters that are responsible for most mental disorders are:

- Dopamine
- Serotonin
- Norepinephrine

Besides these neurotransmitters, there are others that also send messages in a person's brain. These include; GABA, acetylcholine, and glutamate. Scientists are still studying the specifics of what role these chemicals play in the brain when it comes to a person's depression or other mental conditions like fibromyalgia and Alzheimer's.

Let's learn a little about how our cells communicate with our neurotransmitters. A synapse is a space between two nerve cells. When two cells want to communicate with each other, our neurotransmitters can be packed up and then released from the cell for the destined cell to receive. As these packaged neurotransmitters travel across the space, postsynaptic cells can take up those receptors if they are looking for a specific chemical.

For instance, serotonin receptors will aim to pick up serotonin molecules. If there are any excess lingering molecules in that space, the presynaptic cell will gather those molecules and use them in another communication by reprocessing them. Different types of neurotransmitters carry different messages that play a specific role in the creation of a person's brain chemistry. Imbalanced in those chemicals are theorized to play a huge role in depression or other mental health conditions.

Chapter 3: Phobias

Phobia disorders are probably one of the most well-known anxiety disorders in the world. You constantly see phobias being displayed in media such as movies about clowns, heights, or spiders. Keep in mind that fear and concern regarding specific situations is completely normal and does not mean that you have a phobia. For example, if you are scared of spiders, it doesn't mean you have a phobia. However, if you revolve your life around making sure there are no spiders, then you likely have a phobia. In normal circumstances, fear is a rational and natural response in our bodies when we feel threatened.

What is a Phobia Disorder?

Those who suffer from a phobia disorder will have a huge reaction when it comes to certain situations, activities, or objects. This is due to them exaggerating the danger in their heads. The terror, panic, and fear that they feel are completely blown out of proportion. In severe cases, an individual who has a phobia disorder may have a big reaction by just seeing their phobic stimulus on TV. People who have these extreme reactions often are suffering from a specific phobia disorder.

Most people who suffer from anxiety or anxiety disorders are typically not aware of where their anxiety is coming from. On the contrary, people who suffer from phobia disorder is very aware of what their fears are and how it's irrational and extreme. However, they feel like their fear is automatic and is not something that can be controlled or reduced. In serious cases of phobia disorders, it could lead to panic attacks. This increases the likelihood of this individual, also developing a panic disorder as well. The following are symptoms of a phobia disorder:

- An irrational, constant, and extreme fear of a specific situation, object, or activity. (e.g., the fear of spiders, dogs, or water).

- Constant avoidance of situations where there is a possibility of encountering a phobia. (e.g., not going outside because you may encounter a dog).

- Constant avoidance and anxiety regarding specific situations make it difficult for the individual to go about their daily routine. (e.g. not going outside because you may encounter a dog which causes you to miss important things like work/school).

- Avoidance and anxiety is constant and is lasting for 6 months + .

The first symptoms of phobia disorder usually arise during childhood or early adolescence. Fear is normal throughout childhood, and children often share common fears like; strangers, the dark, imaginary monsters, and animals. However, the process of growing up is learning to manage these fears properly. Children who never learned to properly deal with their fears are at a higher risk of developing phobia disorder in their adulthood. Some children have such severe phobias that develop into panic attacks later on. This demographic has a higher chance of developing other types of anxiety disorders in their adult life.

Many different factors contribute to the development of a phobia disorder. First of all, a person's temperament and mental health history are the biggest players in the development of a phobia disorder. Fortunately, phobias are one of the more treatable disorders, and treatments like Cognitive Behavioral Therapy is the first form of treatment used to tackle this disorder. Medication will be used to treat phobia disorder in more severe cases but is likely partnered with CBT as well.

Types of Phobias

There are endless amounts of phobia types. Types of phobia disorders are usually split into the following categories:

- Animals: Your fear is related to animals or insects (e.g., fear of cats or spiders).

- Natural environment: Your fear is related to the natural environment (e.g., fear of heights or lightning).

- Injury/injection: Your fear is related to invasive medical procedures (e.g., fear of needles or seeing blood)

- Situations: Your fear is related to very specific situations (e.g., riding an escalator or driving in busy traffic).

- Other: Your fear is related to miscellaneous phobias (e.g., fear of throwing up or fear of choking).

How Do Phobias Develop?

We know thus far that phobias are likely developed due to anxiety disorders. However, scientists have been studying numerous theories and have classified them into three unique categories. These include biological causes, learning-based causes, and psychoanalytic causes. It is unlikely that these causes are mutually exclusive since there is a much higher chance that these causes all interact within a person to cause the birth of a phobia. For instance, a person's cause could be the biological differences in their brain that become triggered by an experience in their environment; that negative experience they just witnessed may cause them to have a 'learned response'.

Let's take a look into three different theories.

1. Psychoanalytic Theory

This theory is based on Sigmund Freud as he pioneered the theory of the three stages of conscience within a person: These are Id, Ego, and Superego. The Id is the most instinctual aspect of the mind and is the foundation of our primitive emotions; anxiety and fear. The superego is a higher conscience that is selfless and values concepts of guilt and judgments. Lastly, the ego is there to control the Id's impulses. According to the psychoanalytic theory, phobias are created based on the Id's anxiety reactions that have been repressed by one's ego. In simpler terms, the object that is currently feared was not the original subject of the fear.

2. <u>Learning Theory</u>

This theory is based on a set of theories that are related to cognitive theory and behaviorism. Ivan Pavlov spearheaded the learning theory by doing an experiment that proved that dogs could be trained to salivate when a certain bell was rung. After that, other psychologists used this study to build numerous other theories based on human behavior. Based on this theory, phobias are developed when a person's fear response is punished or reinforced.

3. <u>Biological Basis</u>

This theory is based on a medical model of psychology. This means that this model supports the theory that phobias are caused by physiological factors. Neuropsychologists in this field have found multiple genetic factors that play a role in a person's development of phobias.

This research started very recently, but it has already found that certain medications have been useful in treating one's phobias. Many of these medical treatments work by relieving anxiety by increasing serotonin levels.

Common Phobias

Phobia disorders are becoming more and more apparent in our society today. Most movies and TV shows portray phobias in the form of spiders, clowns, and tall heights. However, some of the most common phobias are much less tangible than the Hollywood embellished ones that we are used to. Let's take a look at ten of the most common phobias in our society today.

1. Social Phobias

This fits into our topic perfectly; social phobias are the #1 most common phobias in our society today. This is classified as a social anxiety disorder, and the main symptom is the excessive self-consciousness that a person feels during social interactions. Some people may have a social phobia so bad that they are afraid of eating in front of people.

2. <u>Agoraphobia</u>

This is the fear of open spaces. This is a very serious phobia that can cause people to be trapped in their homes, which makes their ability to live a normal life very difficult to achieve. Although the severity levels in people differ greatly, most people who have this may avoid specific open-space venues or places.

3. <u>Acrophobia</u>

This is the fear of heights. Some people have such a strong fear of heights that even riding in escalators at a shopping mall can make them nauseous or give them vertigo. Vertigo is a medical condition where people can develop dizziness so bad that they throw up and pass out. For less severe types, acrophobia could be experiencing faintness when you are standing at the top of a tall cliff or looking out of a skyscraper.

4. Pteromerhanophobia

With the increased news coverage of crashed airplanes, it is understandable that many people fear flying on an airplane. However, the chances of this happening are actually quite low, but it does not stop people from being afraid.

5. Claustrophobia

Claustrophobia is a fear that we commonly hear about and is defined as the fear of enclosed spaces. People who suffer from this phobia often feel as if the walls around them are closing in. There are theories that suggest that there is a genetic link for claustrophobia as some type of human survival mechanism.

6. Entomophobia

Entomophobia is the fear of insects and is one that is seen commonly in everyday life. However, being afraid of an insect flying past you is not the same as being so afraid that you won't leave your home in the fear of encountering an insect.

7. Ophidiophobia

Ophidiophobia is the fear of snakes and is also one that is commonly heard of in everyday life. Just like entomophobia, being afraid of a snake when you are out camping is not the same as being so afraid of snakes that you refuse to go anywhere with grass or nature.

8. Cynophobia

Cynophobia is the fear of dogs and is quite common amongst kids and people who work in door-to-door professions like mailmen. This fear seems to be developed by previous negative experiences and is one of the hardest phobias out there to conquer. Since dogs can sense people's fear, they may act more aggressively to those that are afraid of them, causing their phobia to worsen.

9. Astraphobia

Astraphobia is the fear of storms; this is typically towards loud storms such as lightning storms. The actual fear, in this case, is the actual lightning striking you and causing death, but the chance of that happening is very, very slim.

10. Trypanophobia

Trypanophobia is the fear of needles. Many people develop this fear when they are young during doctor's appointments. However, needles typically aren't that painful, and if they are, they are worth the pain in order to ensure good health.

Treatments of Phobias

As mentioned earlier, diagnosing whether or not you have a phobia disorder is based on completing clinical interviews and diagnostic guidelines performed by a licensed professional. The doctor will ask questions regarding your symptoms and look into your social, medical, and psychiatric history. They may follow the criteria of the Diagnostic and Statistical Manual of Mental Disorders (DSM-5), or they may follow a different set of criteria. Once the diagnosis is complete, the doctor will recommend the best form of treatment for your specific case.

When it comes to treatment for phobias, the best form of treatment on the market right now is exposure therapy. Other doctors could recommend different forms, but this is the one that is most commonly recommended. The purpose of treatment is to help a person with a phobia disorder to improve their quality of life so that they no longer have to live a life that is revolved around their fears. You can better learn how to manage your feelings, thoughts, and reactions so that your anxieties and fears are no longer controlling your life. Treatment is often focused on one specific phobia at a time. Let's take a look at two different types of psychotherapy aimed at treating phobia disorders:

1. Exposure Therapy

Exposure therapy focuses on helping a person change their response to the situation or object that they fear. It is done in a gradual and repeated manner where they expose you to your specific phobia. This is all based on the fact that the thoughts, feelings, and behaviors generated by being exposed to your phobia can help you learn to manage your feelings of anxiety.

For instance, if you are afraid of riding in cars, your exposure therapy may start with you simply just thinking about getting into a car. As you get a better handle on that thought, you can move on to looking at photos of cars to standing near a car, to actually sitting into one that isn't moving. Once you are comfortable with those behaviors, you can then take a ride in a car that's moving very slowly with no other cars around to then riding in a car normally through traffic.

2. Cognitive Behavioral Therapy

Cognitive Behavioral Therapy is a treatment method that helped you look at and cope with your feared object/situation differently. Throughout this therapy, you will learn different beliefs regarding your fears and how it has impacted your life. CBT focuses on the fact that a person's thoughts control their emotions, which control their behaviors. By changing your thoughts around a certain subject, you have the ability to control your emotions and, thus, manage your actions towards it.

Most of the time, psychotherapy is very effective when it comes to treating people with phobia disorders. However, certain medications can help reduce the anxiety symptoms of a person that is experiencing their phobia. Most medications are recommended for use during very specific situations that happen infrequently. For instance, medication might be prescribed for those that are about to go on a flight but have a fear of flying. Here are two medications that are recommended for phobias:

1. Beta-Blockers

This type of drug blocks the effects of adrenaline, which is normally produced when a person is experiencing fear or anxiety. This helps reduce the symptoms of anxiety such as a racing heart, elevated blood pressure, and shaky limbs and voice.

2. Sedatives

Drugs such as benzodiazepines help people relax but reducing their anxiety levels. These drugs are a type of sedative and need to be used very carefully as of their highly addictive nature. This drug should be avoided by those who have a history of drug or alcohol abuse.

Chapter 4: The Test

The Liebowitz Social Anxiety Scale is a test that a health professional may ask a patient to do if they suspect that they have social anxiety. This test measures the amount of influence that a social anxiety disorder has in your life by asking about a variety of situations. The test will provide you with numerous different social situations, and then it will measure how your response scores.

It uses two types of measurements; first, it will ask you how much you fear that situation. Second, it will ask you how often you avoid that situation. If you come across a situation that you have never really experienced, or don't experience often, you will rate the situation based on the hypothetical situation. In simpler terms, you rate how you think you would feel about the situation and how likely you would avoid it.

The Liebowitz Social Anxiety Scale Test

Every situation needs to be rated from 0 – 3. 0 means no fear, 1 means mild fear, 2 means moderate fear, and 3 means severe fear. Avoidance is also rated from 0 – 3. 0 means never, 1 means occasionally, 2 means often, and 3 means usually. In order to get an idea of your social anxiety severity, please complete the test below.

Situation	Fear (0 – 3)	Avoidance (0 – 3)
Using a phone in public spaces		
Participating in a small group activity		
Eating in public		
Drinking with other people		
Talking to an authority figure		

Situation	Fear (0 – 3)	Avoidance (0 – 3)
Speaking, acting or performing in front of others		
Going to a party		
Working while being watched		
Writing will be watched		
Calling someone whom you don't know very well		
Talking in-person with someone whom you don't know very well		
Meeting strangers		
Urinating in a public bathroom		
Entering a room when others are already seated		

Situation	Fear (0 – 3)	Avoidance (0 – 3)
Being the center of attention		
Speaking up at a meeting		
Taking a test regarding your knowledge, skill, or ability		
Expressing disapproval or disagreement with someone whom you don't know very well		
Maintaining eye contact with someone that you don't know very well		
Giving a prepared speech to a group of people		
Trying to acquaint someone for the purpose of a romantic/sexual relationship		

Situation	Fear (0 – 3)	Avoidance (0 – 3)
Returning goods to a store for a refund		
Giving a party		
Resisting a salesperson that is high-pressure and pushy		

What Do the Range of Scores Mean?

Once you have completed this test, let's take a look at what the range of scores means. Sum up your score from both columns. If you scored anywhere between 0 – 29, you are someone who does not suffer from social anxiety. This mostly means that you feel anxious occasionally during social situations, which are completely normal. Nobody lives their life feeling zero anxiety at all, that is just not possible.

If you scored between 30 – 49, you have mild social anxiety. This means that you do suffer from social anxiety, but likely not enough of it to hinder you from carrying on with your daily routine and life duties. This is someone who may avoid social situations if he/she can but can overcome it enough if he/she knows that they need to get something done.

If you scored between 50 – 64, then you have moderate social anxiety. This is probably the most common form of social anxiety where you would likely opt out of every social situation if you can but will struggle through it if you know it needs to be done. Your life may be slightly hindered due to your social anxiety but not affected to the point where you can't go on with your day to day routine.

If you scored between 65 – 79, then you have marked social anxiety. This is pretty high and would likely require treatment immediately before it manifests into other types of mental disorders. Someone with this level of social anxiety may try to avoid social situations at all costs, even if he/she knows it will hinder their life. This person is at risk of developing other types of disorders such as depression or GAD.

If you scored between 80 – 94, then you have severe social anxiety. This is very high, and a person suffering from this is likely making an effort to avoid any type of social situation. People with severe social anxiety tend to isolate themselves by staying at home and struggle to live a normal and healthy life due to the fear of encountering people out in the world. They are at a high risk of developing other mental disorders as well.

If you scored 95+, then you have very severe social anxiety. This is extremely high, and you are likely living a very unhealthy life if this is the case. You may be avoiding leaving your home in fear that you may run into people, and any thought of social interactions create overwhelming anxiety for you. If this is your score, please reach out to your support network to get professional help immediately.

Chapter 5: Self-Help Strategies to Cope With Social Anxiety

Before we learn about prescribed treatment methods like psychotherapy and medication, let's take a look at self-help strategies that could be used to help improve one's social anxiety. These self-help strategies can be used before seeking professional treatment or during it as well. I encourage you to continuously practice self-coping skills that you have learned even if you are in the process of receiving professional treatment. This is important as the more treatment methods you employ, the more effective it is in helping you reduce the amount of social anxiety you feel.

In this chapter, we will be studying two types of coping; social coping and emotional coping. Social coping encompasses learning better communication skills in order to better cope with functioning in social situations. Emotional coping consists of reducing negative thinking, coming to terms with your fears, and breathing exercises that can help calm you down during high-anxiety moments. Let's take a look at each.

Social Coping

As we just mentioned, social coping helps you by improving your communication skills to make navigating social situations much easier. People who suffer from social anxiety may have also developed inefficient communication skills in the process. They often struggle with boundaries, assertiveness, and verbal communication. Social coping can help people feel less anxious in social situations by teaching them the right communication skills to help them feel more confident around others. Within this subchapter, we will be looking at improving one's assertiveness, non-verbal communication, verbal communication, and the importance of utilizing your support network.

Improving Assertiveness

Assertiveness is something that is absolutely required to live a healthy life. Self-esteem is responsible for increasing one's assertiveness. It helps with this by creating a strong belief in the things you are saying, doing, and asking. If an individual believes that they need or want something, they often don't spend any time dwelling on if people think it is true. Instead, they just ask for it.

Individuals that have low self-esteem often have trouble with assertiveness because of the fear of being rejected or judged. They often think that asking for something they need is a sign of weakness, and therefore, they will be judged for simply asking. On the other hand, an individual with healthy self-esteem isn't afraid of asking for what they need because that thought of doubt simply doesn't cross their mind.

Often, those with social anxiety will go along with everything that others say and don't often express their opinions or thoughts. This makes social encounters more difficult to navigate as it is tiring to constantly have to agree with everyone else or go along with everything that others say. Improving your assertiveness is an effective way of expressing yourself in front of others.

Don't get this confused with aggressiveness; you don't need to be aggressive to be assertive. In order to improve your own assertiveness, you must improve your self-esteem. Without self-esteem, assertiveness is something that is difficult to do since you do not place a priority on your own needs. Increasing your self-esteem will, in turn, increase your assertiveness, which will improve your ability to cope during social situations.

Here's another example of assertiveness; this time, the example will be in the place of work. Imagine if your manager just asked you for the fourth time this month to step in and complete your co-worker's deliverable because she has fallen behind schedule yet once again and knows that you are a more efficient employee than her. Someone with healthy self-esteem will respond with assertiveness like "This is the fourth time in the month that I have taken on extra work because Jessica is behind schedule, again. I highly value being a team player, but I feel stressed when I am overwhelmed with extra work. What can we do to make sure this doesn't happen so often?".

That is the ideal way to respond to your manager in a situation like this because you have to have enough respect yourself to tell them that enough is enough. A person with low self-esteem in this situation will likely agree to take on the extra work and end up resenting their coworker for it. They may drain themselves too much by doing more work and blame other people for it, thus creating unhealthy relationships. By communicating with others to let them know your feelings and needs will give them an opportunity to understand and adjust their own actions accordingly.

For a socially anxious person, the example above could've easily sent him/her into a spiral of self-doubt, anxiety, and maybe even depression. However, if you begin working on your self-esteem to foster more assertiveness, these situations are all ones that can easily be dealt with by simply communicating your thoughts in a clear and assertive manner. If he/she is unable to do this, they will feel more socially anxious as they will try to avoid the situation rather than just responding to it. They may end up avoiding work just so they don't have to confront their boss about not wanting to pick up their coworkers slack.

Learning to be assertive is a life skill that is important due to how often it is used and respected. If you think you are suffering from the "yes" syndrome, your first step may be to work on your self-esteem to help you respect your own wants and needs. Take into consideration, however, that being assertive is not the same as being aggressive. Many people avoid being assertive as they confuse it with aggression. Assertiveness means to be firm and clear about what one needs/wants, while aggression is a harsh demand. The way you deliver your message using body language and tone of voice influences how people perceive your request.

Improving Non-Verbal Communication

Those who are socially anxious often misread other people's non-verbal communication, which creates more anxiety for themselves. By learning to read other people's non-verbal communication, they can make a more informed assessment about the people in the social situation they're in. For instance, they may think that someone is angry with them because their arms are crossed when really, the person may be angry with someone else, or they're stressed at an external factor. Nonverbal communication factors into a large percentage of what humans' base their first impressions of others on. Because of this, it is very important to understand what the things we see are telling us.

We can learn a lot about a person before speaking a word to them by simply examining their nonverbal actions. We do this already in our day-to-day life simply because we are visual creatures. Our eyes perceive the world around us, and this is no different when perceiving people. Because of this, everyone including you already has a foundation to begin reading nonverbal communication in a more focused and specific way. Learning what to look for and how to decipher this type of communication involves fine-tuning a skill that each of us already possesses. You can almost quickly profile anybody just by assessing their nonverbal communication skills. Let's take a look at the different components of non-verbal communication and what they mean.

- <u>The Eyes</u>

Firstly, the eyes. Our eyes operate greatly on their own accord- blinking when they need to and gazing where there is movement. While we can most often control where they look, they will sometimes operate on their own in interactions with others. The eyes will often be the first place to show how the person is feeling. Our brain and our spinal cord make up the pairing that is known as the central nervous system. This pathway of neurons operates fully automatically- that is to say, with no help from our conscious mind. The eyes are connected to this nervous system and are the only part of the central nervous system that actually faces the outside of the body.

Because of this, the eyes are literally intertwined with what we are thinking and feeling, even more than we notice. The brain and the spinal cord give us life- they are responsible for initiating our movements, our thoughts, and our feelings. "The eyes are the window to the soul" got its origins in this fact of anatomy. That being said, it is very difficult to control the emotions and sentiments that people can see in our eyes as they come directly from the places within us over which we have no control. The eyes, therefore, are the first place to look when it comes to seeing someone's truth.

Eye movement is also a type of communication that goes on. The eyes tend to go where the person wants to go. If someone glances at something, chances are they are thinking about it or wishing to go there. For example, if someone glances at a chair in the room, they are probably tired of standing. If someone glances at the door, they would probably like to leave or they may be late for something. If you see someone looking over at another table for the duration of your dinner date, chances are they wish they were with someone else.

Think of yourself in this type of situation. On a date where you feel bored and unenthused, you would probably be searching wildly around the room for an excuse to leave or another person to daydream about. If your date is unaware of what your eye movements are demonstrating, they may keep droning on about the stock market for another hour or two.

While everyone blinks at slightly different rates, you can start to pick up on changes in blinking speed. Watch your partner next time they are sitting across from you and notice how often they blink. Picking up on this will alert you when there is a change in blinking speed. Blinking very often and quickly is said to be an indicator of thinking hard or of stress. What causes your partner to begin blinking quickly? This observation will give you some insight into what causes them stress and mental strain.

- <u>The Mouth</u>

Another place to look on the face is the mouth. The mouth's subtle movements often go completely unnoticed by the person themselves. We will examine a smile, for instance. A genuine smile will include a change or movement in all parts of the face; this happens automatically and is not controlled by the person. A fake smile, however, will only involve the movement of the mouth into the desired shape of a smile and not involve the eyes or the upper areas of the face. These two types of smiles can tell a great deal about what a person is thinking.

A real and genuine smile indicates that the person is happy and interested, while a fake smile indicates that the person wants approval or acceptance. Another type of smile is one that includes the movement of only one side of the mouth. This type indicates that the person is feeling unsure or not convinced.

- <u>Facial Expressions</u>

Subtle movements of the face can be picked up when examining another person closely. These subtle movements are said to happen instinctively when a person has a feeling of intense emotion. They are very difficult to fake as they happen quickly and subtly. These subtle movements can be very telling if we can learn to pick up on them.

The first involuntary facial movement is that of **surprise**. When genuinely surprised, a human face will drop the jaw, raise the eyebrows and widen the eyes. The second is **fear**. Fear causes the eyebrows to rise slightly, the upper eyelid to raise, and the lips to tense. The next is **disgust**, which causes the upper lip to rise and the nose to wrinkle. **Anger** causes the eyebrows to lower, the lips to come together, and the bottom jaw to come forward. **Happiness** causes the corners of the lips to rise, the cheeks to rise, and the outsides of the eyes to wrinkle. This wrinkling of the eyes is indicative of a real smile, in a fake smile, this does not happen. **Sadness** involves the outside of the lips to lower, the inside of the eyebrows to raise and the lower lip to come forward. Finally, an intense feeling of **hate** causes one side of the mouth to raise.

These expressions all take place so quickly that they are often missed. If you know what to look for though, you will notice them before they are gone. This will be one of the most accurate ways to analyze a person as they will likely have no idea that this has occurred on their face.

- The Arms

First is the movement of the arms. The arms themselves can close us off or open us up to the world. The positioning of the arms in relation to the body can be something that happens automatically. Someone may be extremely comfortable with the situation they are in if they have their arms at their sides, resting on the armrests of the chair in which they are seated. This may happen automatically as a result of feeling unthreatened and safe in their surroundings.

A person may cross their arms when they are feeling threatened or hug their chest in an effort to protect themselves from the outside world. When people do this, they are attempting to physically put a barrier between themselves and you, whether they know this to be true or not. Our bodies are made to automatically protect us from danger. Our emotions and feelings signal to our body that there may be a threat and our body acts accordingly. This happens regardless of whether there is a real physical threat, or simply a topic of conversation that is making is uncomfortable. To our brain, it is all the same.

When someone is feeling comfortable and welcoming, they may open their arms and leave themselves fully open to receiving the world.

Arms behind the back indicate that the person is feeling secure and welcoming a challenge. We know this because they have their protecting elements (their arms) behind them and their chest out and exposed, meaning that they will not be able to quickly protect themselves if need be. This is an indication of feeling secure and comfortable or feeling like they are stronger than those around them.

- The Hands

The hands being up around the face indicates a desire to remain mysterious or not to show one's true expressions.

Hands on hips may indicate that a person is trying to assert dominance. When someone puts their hands on their hips, it makes them take up much more space. Putting the hands on the hips is usually accompanied by a wide stance. This type of body positioning causes people to spread themselves out as if to say, "you can try to cross me, but it will not work."

Hands in the pockets can indicate nervousness and even deceitful behavior as they are hiding a part of themselves that tends to move in an indicative way. Look out for this along with other signals that the person may be trying to withhold information or remain vague.

The hands holding something between the person and you create another type of barrier like crossing the arms does. For example, holding a book or a notepad out in front of them is putting something between themselves and you in order to distance themselves from the conversation. this can indicate unease or a lack of openness, which can translate to their words being distant or reserved.

- <u>The Feet</u>

The feet are another important place to look in order to analyze a person. This is because people are usually expecting their face to be the place people look to for clues into their subconscious, so they forget all about their feet placement. The feet placement is similar to the glance mentioned earlier in that it tells you where the person wants to be. Just as someone will glance in the direction of what they want, their feet will usually point in the direction of where they want to be.

If someone is talking to you, but their feet are pointing to the restroom, they may be trying to find a moment to exit and take care of their business. If their feet are pointing at someone else, chances are they would rather be talking to them. If their feet are pointing to you, they are engaged in your conversation and would not rather be elsewhere at that moment. This can tell you about someone's intentions and paired with their facial expression or arm placement; you can determine their motives.

Developing Verbal Communication

Being able to assess other people's feelings through analyzing their non-verbal communication is important. What's equally as important, however, especially for a socially anxious person, is knowing the proper and most effective communication techniques. The ability to communicate effectively and creating positive responses from others can improve the confidence of a socially anxious person greatly. Let's take a look at what effective communication is and how to execute it.

Let's take a look at the term "effective communication." What exactly is effective communication? Effective communication is essentially a combination of verbal communication and non-verbal communication portrayed in a manner that is well-received by others. Effective communication is built up of these seven points:

1. The ability to listen effectively and actively
2. The ability to observe your own thoughts and feelings
3. The ability to know when a response is needed and when it is not
4. The ability to observe other people's words and actions and practice empathy
5. The ability to form thoughtful and appropriate responses according to your observations of yourself and others, through empathy
6. The ability to deliver your words or actions in a clear manner so that they can be easily understood

7. The ability to speak in an articulate manner with effective choice of words

When trying to determine whether you are an effective communicator or whether you need to work on your communication skills, you can look at the frequency with which misunderstandings occur in your relationships and interactions. This is a good indication of how effectively you are able to listen and to speak, as the more effective your communication skills, the fewer misunderstandings you should have.

You may be saying, "but what if I am a great communicator, but the other person is not?" If this is the case, you should still be able to listen actively in order to ask for clarification where needed, thus allowing you to resolve any possible misunderstandings or miscommunications. Even if the other person needs to work on their communication skills, if you are an effective communicator, you should be able to effectively direct the interaction in order to get the information you need from the person. You should also be able to speak in a clear and articulate manner so that you are able to effectively get your points across and ensure that you are not being misunderstood.

By improving upon the seven points above, social situations will feel less daunting as you are confident in your ability to navigate through it.

If you are interested in improving your communication skills, I wrote a book on the subject that you can find on Amazon. Go to the last page of this book and you will find the direct link.

Utilizing Your Support Network

The last topic we are going to talk about within social coping is the importance of utilizing your support network. Even the most socially anxious person has at least one person that they are comfortable communicating with. Use them and confide in them. By isolating yourself completely, you are making it more difficult to get back out in society. Reach out to whoever is within your support network and ask for support.

This can be in the form of simply just chatting, going to social outings together, or having someone to be there for you when you are practicing coping methods. Let go of any judgment that you have for yourself and others and let yourself be vulnerable. You may be surprised to find out how many people are willing to help you overcome your problems.

Emotional Coping

Emotional coping helps you by relaxing you during moments of high-anxiety. For instance, if you were feeling extremely anxious before you go to a work event, you may want to have a few coping methods ready in case you need to use them then and there. Emotional coping methods are normally used as a recovery measure during times of high-anxiety to prevent panic attacks. In this subchapter, we will be studying breathing exercises, reducing negative thinking, confronting your fears, and what situations to avoid.

Breathing Exercises

Breathing exercises are a good way to maintain low levels of anxiety and also help calm you down when you are having extreme bouts of anxiety. Breathing is a necessity of life that we often don't think too much about. When a person breathes in the air, their blood cells receive oxygen and then release carbon dioxide. Carbon dioxide is a waste product that is exhaled. Breathing improperly can mix up the oxygen and carbon dioxide exchange and can contribute to conditions like panic attacks, anxiety, and fatigue.

Many people are not conscious of how they are breathing. There are two types of general breathing patterns, thoracic (chest) breathing and diaphragmatic (abdominal) breathing. Anxious people tend to breathe rapidly and shallowly directly from their chests. This is thoracic breathing. Most people, when they are anxious, are unaware that they are breathing this way. Thoracic breathing causes a disrupt between the levels of oxygen and carbon dioxide, which results in muscle tension, increased heart rate, and dizziness.

When your blood is not absorbing the right amounts of oxygen, it may signal a stress response that triggers panic attacks. By using diaphragmatic breathing; instead, you mimic the way newborn babies breathe and the way you breathe when you are in a stage of deep and relaxed sleep.

The best way to determine which breathing pattern you are doing is to place one hand on your upper abdomen and the other hand in the middle of your chest. When you breathe, pay attention to which hand is raised the most. If you are breathing properly, your hand on the abdomen should rise the most. Be aware of these differences during times of stress and anxiety because these are the times where you are most likely to breathe from your chest.

Here is a simple relaxation technique to help you the next time you are feeling anxious:

1. **Inhale** in a slow and deep manner using your nose. Relax your shoulders, and your abdomen should expand while your chest rises minimally.

2. **Exhale** slowly through your lips. As you are blowing the air out, purse your lips a little bit while keeping your jaw relaxed. You may hear a "whooshing" sound as you exhale.

3. **Repeat** this exercise for several minutes.

People who are diagnosed with panic disorder may feel more anxious or panicked during this breathing exercise. It is likely due to the anxiety that is caused by focusing on breathing (a symptom of panic attacks). You may not be able to do this exercise correctly right off the bat and may need some practice for it to work. If you find that it is creating more anxiety or panic for you, stop for now. Try it again in a day or two to build up the time gradually.

Reduce Negative Thinking

One of the most effective therapy methods to treat social anxiety is Cognitive Behavioral Therapy. A huge component of CBT focuses around reducing negative thinking by helping the patient become more aware of their own unhelpful thinking styles (or otherwise known as cognitive distortions). We will spend more time talking about CBT later on in this book.

In order to reduce your own negative thinking, you first have to learn and understand the numerous types of unhelpful thinking styles. By learning what the different types of styles are, you will learn what to look out for to identify when you are participating in those unhelpful thinking styles. If you learn how to determine whether your worry is justified or not, you will be able to control your worry when it isn't justified. Here are twelve different types of cognitive distortions that you need to know:

1. <u>All or nothing thinking</u>: This is also known as 'black and white thinking'. This type of

thinking style leads people to see everything in only success or failure, or black and white. If something isn't perfect, it is deemed a failure.

2. <u>Overgeneralization</u>: This is when an individual sees one single negative event as a continuous pattern. The individual will draw conclusions of future situations based on a singular situation.

3. <u>Mental filter</u>: This individual will pick one unfavorable detail and dwell on it exclusively. The individual begins to perceive reality negatively. They don't notice their successes and only focuses on their failures.

4. <u>Disqualifying the positive</u>: The individual discounts their successes and/or positive experiences by claiming that it "doesn't count." By discounting everything positive, the individual maintains a negative perspective even if their daily life contradicts it.

5. Jumping to conclusions: The individual will make a negative assumption without having supporting evidence. There are two different types of jumping to conclusions:

    a. Mind reading: The individual imagines that they already know what others are having negative thoughts about them. Therefore there's no reason to ask or confirm.

    b. Fortune-telling: The individual predicts that things will end up badly regardless and convinces themselves that their prediction is a fact.

6. Magnification/Minimization: The individual blows negative situations out of proportion or shrinks positive situations to make it appear insignificant. For instance, the individual exaggerates somebody else's success (magnification) and does not credit their own success (minimization).

7. Catastrophizing: The individual associates extreme and disastrous consequences to the outcome of certain situations. For instance, if the individual asks someone out for a date and is rejected, they believe that they are going to be alone forever.

8. Emotional reasoning: The individual makes an assumption that their negative emotions are reflective of reality. For example, "I feel disliked, so, therefore, I am".

9. "Should statements": The individual uses "should" and "shouldn't" statements to motivate themselves. They associate rewards and punishment with these statements. Individuals are angered if other people do not follow their "should" and "shouldn't" statements.

10. Labeling and mislabeling: The individual overgeneralizes things to the extreme. Rather than analyzing their mistakes, they automatically label something negative to themselves. For example, if they failed a

work assignment, then they are a "loser." Often, individuals also do this to others by determining which behavior of others isn't desirable and attaching "they are a loser" to them.

11. <u>Personalization</u>: The individual takes responsibility for things that aren't their fault. They will often see themselves as the cause of an external situation.

12. <u>All at once, bias</u>: The individual will think that there are an increasing amount of risk and threats right at their front door. When this happens, individuals begin to:

   a. Believe that negative events are happening quicker than you can come up with solutions.

   b. Think that situations are moving too quickly and begin to feel overwhelmed.

   c. Think that there is little time between now and the oncoming threat.

d. Think that numerous threats and risks all appear at once.

By learning and understanding what these unhelpful thinking styles are, individuals can begin to interrupt the process when they identify it and say, for example, "I'm magnifying the situation again." When an individual learns to interrupt their own cognitive distortions, they can begin to rebuild it into something that is helpful rather than detrimental. In the next subchapter, we will be learning how an individual can manage their anxiety by challenging these unhelpful thinking styles.

Face Your Fears

Many people that suffer from social anxiety often have many fears, some irrational, some rational. Fear is powerful, helpful, and human emotion. It is the feeling that alerts us when we are in the presence of danger and has been crucial in keeping our species alive. There are two types of responses when it comes to fear; biochemical and emotional. The biochemical response is the universal response of fear, while an emotional response is specific to the individual.

Just like what we learned about anxiety, fear is a natural emotion and a survival mechanism within humans. When humans are confronted with a perceived threat, our bodies will react in specific ways. These physical reactions include increased heart rate, sweating, and high adrenaline levels. Just like how anxiety activates our fight or flight response, fear does too. This is where our body prepares itself to run away or enter combat. These reactions are all biochemical and are an automatic response that has been crucial to our survival. Here are 6 steps that you can follow to begin to tackle your fears:

1. Define your fear.

If you are keeping your fear undefined and foggy, your mind will often make the fear grow stronger over time and continue to hold you back. Instead, sit down with a piece of paper and a pen and write out what your fear actually is as specific as you can. This exercise will help you bring clarity to what you fear, defuse any disaster scenarios you may have, and help you realize that you can bounce back quickly even if your worst-case scenario actually happens.

2. Share your fear.

When you keep your fears to yourself, then it can easily manifest into something horrific due to your imagination and create something that is worse than it seems. Sharing your fears with someone else will give you an objective opinion on your fear. Since overcoming fear requires an individual to change their perspective, I encourage you to talk to other family and friends about your fear and exchange ideas and experiences about your perceived fear to help deflate it.

3. Change your perspective.

If an individual is only focusing on the negative things that will happen if confronted by their fear, it will become difficult to move on from it. Instead, changing your perspective by talking to other people and exchanging experiences can help you realize what other opportunities lie ahead once you overcome your fear. Focus on the positive and think about why you want to move toward and past what you fear.

4. Question your fears.

People who suffer from phobias or irrational fears start to take their experience with their fear as evidence of permanent and frightening fear. However, the smart thing to do would be to question your fears and what they are based upon. Sit down and think back to what evidence you may have in your memories that lead to this fear of yours. When you identify that situation, try to look at it from a new perspective rather than looking at them in the same way. Our minds often jump to conclusions or create patterns based on little evidence or experiences, so by questioning our perspective of fear. You may be able to realize that you were looking at it all wrong this whole time.

5. Don't push your fear away.

When people try to deny their fears, they try to push it out of their lives and to not think about it, which then causes it to grow stronger. Instead, accept your fear and let the discomfort take over you, but after a while, your fear begins to lose steam and becomes a lot smaller in comparison to before. Then, it becomes a lot easier to think of constructive and clear thoughts.

6. Take just one step.

Most people that are heavily affected by fears think that taking action means taking one big and risky leap to overcome that fear. However, thinking about this one big action creates apprehension that often leads to more fear and towards not taking any actions at all. Instead, take just one small step today. Pick up the phone and dial a friend or family for help or just simply read over some exercises to manage your fear. Start small to get the ball rolling.

Things to Avoid

When it comes to avoidance, this is often not encouraged if you are looking to overcome your social anxiety. However, there are certain situations where you're just better off avoiding if possible. For instance, if you have social anxiety and you don't do well in crowds, simply avoid situations where this happens. For instance, if you are planning on going to a concert, don't avoid it altogether just because you're afraid of crowds. Simply purchase your tickets in an area with more open space and fewer crowds, like the lawn area.

The trick here is to avoid situations that make you uncomfortable but not avoiding the whole event altogether. This allows you to start building some resilience and comfortability around social situations whilst avoiding the specific areas which you are anxious about.

Chapter 6: Lifestyle Changes That May Help

On top of utilizing coping techniques and prescribed treatments, lifestyle changes can significantly help those suffering from mental illness. Lifestyle changes may be seemingly simple, but they are actually very powerful tools when it comes to treating social anxiety. In some people's cases, a lifestyle change is all they may need to recover from anxiety. In the case that a person needs other treatment as well, making good lifestyle changes can help cure anxiety even faster and prevent it from happening again.

Here are a few changes that people can try:

- Exercise: Researchers have found that regularly exercising can be just as effective as medication when it comes to treating depression. Exercises boost the 'feel-good' brain chemicals in the brain, such as serotonin and endorphins. These chemicals also trigger the growth of new brain cells and connections similar to what antidepressants and anti-anxiety medication do.

The best part about exercise is that you don't need to do it intensely in order to have the benefits. Even a simple 30-minute walk can make a huge difference in a person's brain activity. For the best results, people should aim to do 30 – 60 minutes of aerobic activity every day or on most days.

- <u>Social Support</u>: Just like I mentioned earlier, having a strong social network reduces isolation, which is a huge risk factor in anxiety. Make an effort to keep in regular contact with family and friends (ideally on a daily basis) and consider joining a support group or class. You can also opt to do some volunteering where you can get the social support you need while helping others as well.

- <u>Nutrition</u>: Eating properly is important for everyone's mental and physical health. By eating well-balanced and small meals throughout the day, it will help you minimize mood swings and keep energy levels up. Although you may crave sugary foods due to the quick boost that they provide, complex carbohydrates are much more nutritious. They can provide you with an energy boost without a crash at the end.

- <u>Sleep</u>: A person's sleep cycle has strong effects on mood. When a person does not get enough sleep, their symptoms of anxiety may get worse. Sleep deprivation causes other negative symptoms like sadness, fatigue, moodiness, and irritability. Not many people can function well with less than seven hours of sleep per night. A healthy adult should be aiming for 7 – 9 hours of sleep every night.

- <u>Stress reduction</u>: When a person is suffering from too much stress, it exacerbates their anxiety and puts them at a higher risk of developing more serious anxiety disorders. Try to make changes in your life that can help you reduce or manage stress. Identify which aspects of your life creates the most stress, such as unhealthy relationships or work overload and find ways to minimize their impact and the stress it brings.

- <u>Quit smoking</u>: Smoking has been proven to increase anxiety and depression levels due to the mixture of chemicals known to be found within cigarettes. In addition, smoking negatively affects a person's health overall, which can increase feelings of anxiety. Although people with social anxiety may indulge in cigarettes hoping to ease their anxiety, it actually does the opposite.

- <u>Avoid Caffeine and limit alcohol</u>: Avoiding caffeine and alcohol is crucial when it comes to treating anxiety and depression. Caffeine and alcohol are both depressants that tend to cause increased heart rate. Since an increased heart rate is a symptom of anxiety, one can easily confuse the symptoms of caffeine with anxiety and make your overall condition worse.

- Add Omega-3: Omega-3 has been proven to improve brain function and has anti-inflammatory benefits. Research has found that omega-3 has numerous benefits for those who are suffering from mental disorders due to the benefits it brings to a person's brain function. Start by consuming more fish and purchasing high omega-3 eggs rather than regular ones.

Meditation/Relaxation Techniques

Mindfulness is also an element in Cognitive Behavioral Therapy but could be utilized on its own through meditation. So what exactly is mindfulness or meditation? Well, mindfulness is a type of meditation that is used as a mental training practice that requires you to focus your mind on your thoughts and sensations in the present moment. Your thoughts include your physical sensations, passing thoughts, and current emotions.

Mindfulness meditation often utilizes mental imagery, breathing practice, muscle and body relaxation, and awareness of your mind and body. For beginners, it is recommended to follow a guided meditation to direct them through the entire process. If there is nobody guiding you through this meditation, it is easy to drift away and fall asleep. That is not the purpose of meditation. When you become more skilled in doing mindfulness meditation, you will be able to do it without a guide or any vocal guidance.

The most original and standardized program for mindfulness meditation is called the Mindfulness-Based Stress Reduction (MSBR) program. This meditation was developed by a Ph.D. student who was a student of a famous Buddhist monk. This program focuses on helping the individual bring their awareness to the present and to focus on their own awareness. This meditation has increased in popularity and is not incorporated into medical settings to treat health conditions such as anxiety, insomnia, pain, and stress.

Although this meditation is quite straightforward, professionals would recommend you to find a teacher or a program that can act as a guide when you begin. Most people are recommended to do this meditation for at least 10 minutes per day. If you don't have a lot of free time, that's okay. Even just a few minutes a day plays a huge role in changing your wellbeing. Follow these instructions below to get started:

1. Find a place that is quiet, and you feel comfortable in. Ideally, this is your home or a place where you feel safe. Sit in something comfortable like a chair and make sure your head and back are straight and aligned. Try to release any tension you feel.

2. Begin to sort your thoughts and put away the ones that are of the past or future. Focus on your thoughts that are about the present.

3. Begin to bring your awareness to your breath. Focus on the sensation of air moving through your body when you inhale and

exhale. Focus on this feeling. Begin to feel the movement of your belly as it rises and falls. Feel how the air enters through your nostrils and leaves through your mouth. Pay attention to how each breath is different.

4. Watch your thoughts come and go in front of you. Pretend you are watching the clouds, letting them slowly pass before you. It doesn't matter if your thought is a worry, anxiety, hope, or fear - when these thoughts pass by, don't ignore them or suppress them. Simply just acknowledge them calmly and anchor yourself by focusing on your breathing.

5. If you find yourself being carried away by your thoughts, observe where your mind drifted off to, and without judging yourself, simply anchor yourself by focusing on your breathing. This happens a lot with beginners, so don't be hard on yourself if you drift away. Always use your breathing as an anchor.

6. When you are nearing the end of your 10-minute session, sit still for two minutes and bring awareness to your physical location. Get up slowly.

Mindfulness meditation is the simplest technique in the meditation field. However, there are other ways of practicing mindfulness that isn't only in the form of meditation. There are a few opportunities in your day where you can use to practice mindfulness. Here are a few suggestions of when you may have the time to practice mindfulness:

1. <u>Doing the dishes</u>: This is a wonderful window of time where you can use to practice mindfulness. Typically, when you are doing the dishes, there isn't anyone trying to get your attention. This is a perfect time to try mindfulness. Try to focus on the feeling of warm water on your hands, the look, and feeling of bubbles, the smell of your dish soap, and the sounds of your plates clunking in the water. Try to give yourself to

this experience and feel your mind refreshing and your anxiety fading.

2. Brushing your teeth: Since you have to brush your teeth every day, you can use this time frame to practice mindfulness. Start by feeling your weight on your feet against the floor, the feeling of your toothbrush in hand, and the movement as you begin to brush your teeth. Focus on these feelings and the thoughts you are having in the present. Don't dwell; just acknowledge those thoughts as they come and go.

3. Driving: This is one of those activities where it's easy for people to do mindlessly. This is especially relevant if you are driving the same route every day. Make use of this time by not letting your mind wander off to think about tasks that you need to do that day. Practice mindfulness by trying to keep yourself anchored. Take in sensations and visuals like the color of the car in front of you, the smell of your own car, and the feeling of the steering wheel. Focus your

attention on all the sounds and noises you hear. If you find yourself wandering, bring your attention back to where you are in your car.

4. Exercising: Make your workout routine a time to also exercise mindfulness. Try to exercise away from screens or music and focus only on your breathing and where your feet are moving. Although watching TV or listening to music will make your workout go by faster or distract you from any anxiety, it won't actually help in managing any unhealthy thoughts. Bring your attention to feeling how your muscles feel and pay attention to how your body is reacting to your workout. Instead of ignoring the pains you may be feeling, acknowledge it, and let yourself feel the exercise.

5. Bedtime: This is normally the time where you begin to get things ready for the next day. Instead of battling too much with it, just keep in mind what needs to be done. Stop trying to rush through it to get to bed, but try

to enjoy the experience of completing those actual tasks. Focus on what needs to be done and don't think about what is next. Start early to leave yourself with enough time, so you don't need to rush through things. Any thoughts or anxieties that come up should be acknowledged and let go.

Help Other People

Helping other people increases one's self-esteem, which produces a positive effect on one's mental health. By helping others, it helps us shift our attention and focus away from ourselves to someone else. Helping others helps us feel grateful for the things that we have, and it feels good to be able to make a difference for someone using your skills. Focusing on yourself is good, especially when you are trying to grow your self-esteem, but helping other people will help your self-esteem grow as well.

According to scientific research, when people help others, the portion of their brain that is responsible for joyful and rewarding feelings becomes activated. That area of the brain that is activated releases the hormones that make us feel good.

What are some ways that you could help others? The simplest and most straightforward way is to just start volunteering in your community. It could be working with children, the homeless, or even just at your local library. This is a good way of gaining some perspective of people that are less fortunate. Often times, some of the things that people are upset with not having, or the constant comparing to others, is immediately gone when you spend some time experiencing how less fortunate people get by. Certain things that people used to be upset about becomes trivial when they gain a new perspective. Here are a few questions to consider when it comes to helping others:

- Do I like being around children, the elderly, or animals?

- How much of my time am I able to offer to others?

- What belongings do I have and no longer need that someone else can benefit from having?

- What skills do I have that local non-profits in my city could use?

- Do I have the financial resources to donate to a nonprofit of my choice?

- What am I generally interested in?

The way you help others doesn't have to be a grand gesture. You can do something very simple, like paying it forward. You can simply leave behind a few dollars for the next person at your local drive-thru or coffee shop. This will make the day for the next person in line. Or you can just take a friend or family member out for dinner for no reason. There are so many little nice things that you can do for others that will help increase your self-esteem.

Find a Sense of Purpose

Finding a sense of purpose can help improve a person's overall mental state. Without purpose, you begin to stop living your life, and you are 'surviving' it instead. Goals help us stay focused and motivated and creates something for people to work towards and look forward to. Begin simply by thinking about what you care about; this could be your family, your pets, or your career. Identify what it is that you are most passionate about in your life and derive your goals from there.

For instance, if you are passionate about animals, you may want to set a goal of starting your own animal shelter or conservatory. It can even be a much smaller goal, like volunteering at the humane society every week. Whatever it is, choosing a goal for yourself helps create a sense of purpose that will motivate you to stay healthy and focused in your life.

Consider Following a Spiritual Path

Following a spiritual path is a method that people have used to manage their mental health. Meditations such as Zen meditation is meant to help uncover a person's innate clarity and workability of the mind. Different from the basic forms of meditation, Zen meditation tackles deep-rooted issues and general life questions that often lack answers. Zen meditation delves deeper than other meditation techniques that focus on relaxation and stress relief. Zen meditation is described as "A special transmission outside the teachings; not established upon words and letters; directly pointing to the human heart-mind; seeing nature and becoming a Buddha" by the famous Buddhist master Bodhidharma.

Zen meditation is often learned and practiced in schools of Zen. They normally practice the sitting meditation called zazen. It begins with sitting upright and following the breath, with an emphasis on the movement within the belly. Traditionally, the practice requires a deep and supportive connection between teacher and pupil. In this case, it would be a Zen master and a dedicated student.

Rather than creating or offering temporary solutions to day to day life problems, Zen meditation aims to address core issues. It explores the true causes of unhappiness and dissatisfaction and redirects our focus in a way that brings about true understanding. In this theory, the true key to happiness and well-being isn't wealth or fame. In fact, the key lies within all of us.

Like other types of spirituality, Buddhism teaches that the more you give, the more you gain. It encourages us to bring awareness of the interconnectedness and appreciation that life gives us, all contained within the present moment. A Zen master might tell you that if you look for inner peace, you won't be able to find it. However, the act of giving up that idea that contains a reward and focusing on other people's happiness will create the possibility for lasting peace.

Although you need to train with a Zen master to understand the complicated depths of this spirituality. I am still able to discuss a few Zen meditation techniques with you. The first is the observation of the breath. The second technique is quiet awareness. Here, the meditator will learn to allow their thoughts to flow through their minds without judging, grasping, or rejecting. There is no particular goal to this technique but to just allow their mind to be. The third technique that Zen meditators use is intensive group meditation. Serious and experienced meditators practice regularly in temples or meditation centers.

Chapter 7: How to Survive Real Life Situations

We learned earlier in this book that communication can be used as a skill to get you through real-life situations. This often includes learning different types of communication, based on whom you are speaking with. For instance, the way you communicate with your boss at work is different from the way you would communicate with your romantic partner. In this chapter, we will be taking a look at different communication methods used based on whom you are speaking with and how you can use communication skills to help you navigate through real-life situations.

Communication is a skill. This is because good communication is something that must be learned and practiced, and is something that not everyone is able to do. Skills are things that one is able to do well and with a high level of ability. This does not usually come naturally and is something that can be learned by anyone.

Communication is one of these things, and if you have the skill of "good communication," this means that you are able to communicate (both giving and receiving information) in an effective and accurate way. This communication involves things that you are feeling, things that you see, or more abstract things like concepts and ideas. This goes hand in hand with emotional intelligence as well, which we will discuss in a further chapter.

Communication in the Workplace

Communication in the workplace means that you are communicating with people whom you have professional relationships with. A professional relationship is very much different than close relationships like friendships and familial relationships. A professional relationship is an ongoing interaction between two individuals that follows a set of established boundaries that are deemed appropriate under their governing standards. The ability to establish professional relationships is the backbone of a person's career development.

Professional relationships consist of many different types. The most common one that people may think of is the relationship that they have with their manager or boss. Or if you are that manager or boss, then professional relationships are the ones you have with your employees. However, professional relationships have many more types than that. Think doctor to patient relationships, lawyer to client, teacher to student, service provider to the customer, and so on and so forth. Professional relationships function in a manner that is very different from friendships and family relationships. Although most professional relationships still have a strong element of friendliness, not many people would consider their doctor their 'friend'.

Professional relationships are one of the most common types of relationships that people struggle with. This is because of how unique it is to the other different types of relationships. If we think about friendships, familial relationships, and romantic relationships, the common element between these three is a level of closeness. When it comes to professional relationships, it is almost forbidden to nurture that sense of closeness. In fact, when two people in a professional relationship grow close, it may evolve into a friendship which overpowers the professional relationship.

Many people have to re-learn their communication skills and techniques solely for professional relationships. Although there isn't a universal mandate for how people should communicate in professional environments, there is a loose structure of how people should act. So why do people give professional relationships so much importance? Why do people take courses or read books on how to build better professional relationships?

The simple answer is that humans are naturally social creatures; we crave positive interactions and friendship as much as we crave food and water. So it does make a lot of sense that the better the relationships we have at work, the happier and more productive we are going to feel. What's more important is that good professional relationships give people more freedom.

Rather than spending time and energy dealing with problems caused by negative relationships, we can simply just focus on our work and opportunities. Good professional relationships are also extremely necessary if you are hoping to develop your career. If your boss or manager doesn't trust you or even like you, then it is highly unlikely that he/she will consider you for a promotion. Overall, people simply want to work with people that they are on good terms with.

Communication With Romantic Partners/Interests

Communication skills literally can make or break your romantic relationships. Let's take a look at how having good (or bad) communication skills can impact your relationships.

If you are a good communicator, this means you are able to:

1. Listen effectively and actively
2. Observe your own thoughts and feelings
3. Know when a response is not needed
4. Observe other people and practice empathy
5. Form thoughtful and appropriate responses according to your observations of yourself and others, through empathy

By being able to do all of these things, you are able to connect with people on a deeper level through understanding. You are able to share information with people effectively and receive information as well. These five points are beneficial in all types of relationships. Relationships are all about connection, and the connection is difficult without the ability to be a good communicator.

If you are a person who struggles with good communication, you may find it difficult to interact with people in professional and personal settings. If you are not able to listen to the people around you and are unable to express yourself through verbal communication, then reaching mutual understanding in your relationships will prove quite difficult. Being able to observe your own thoughts and feelings and explain these to other people through writing or speaking, for example, is very important, and being unable to or ineffective at this can lead to miscommunications or misunderstandings in your relationships.

Bad communication is not always in the form of mean words being exchanged or voices being raised. In most cases, bad communication is a lack of communication. When certain things are not acknowledged or said, both people begin to assume things about one another, and conclusions will be drawn. In order to avoid having bad communication in relationships, over-communication should be used instead. By over-communicating your intentions and your thoughts, the receiving person begins to get an understanding of your style of communication and thought processes. The more they learn about what goes on in your head, the less they will misinterpret you.

This is especially important at the beginning of relationships, as that's where the biggest learning curve is. This holds true not only for romantic relationships, but for professional, personal, and familial relationships as well. Just like how you probably have a strong understanding of the way your best friend thinks and communicates, you should know that you have a weak understanding of the way your new coworker thinks and feels and vice versa. In order to avoid any misunderstandings and arguments, be sure to over-communicate to leave no room for misinterpretations. Once you and the other person have developed an understanding, the two of you can form your own style of communication that works for both parties.

Public Speaking

Public speaking is often done by people who want to influence and persuade. They are likely natural leaders who have mastered the art of communication. This does not mean they don't feel anxious or nervous before a public speech. It just means that they feel are confident in their skills to pull it off. In order to help you with public speaking, we will have to increase your confidence around it. Let's take a look at how learning to persuade and influence people can help you improve our confidence around public speaking.

Being a good public speaker involves some degree of influence and persuasion. When it comes to the type of leadership where there is a vote that decides who the leader will be, persuasion and influence become very important as you will need to get as many people as you can to put their trust in you and select you and what you represent or stand for. Persuasion does not have to include being untruthful, as we have seen that there are many ways to identify if someone is untruthful.

There are other situations where we may want to be influential that does not involve a vote or that are not of a political nature. You may be a parent who needs to influence their child to choose something, or you may want to persuade your friend to make a certain choice. These techniques are still relevant to these types of situations as well.

Appearing confident in your position is crucial when it comes to being persuasive. Just as previously discussed, appearing confident in large part depends on your nonverbal communication. If you think and act like a leader in any situation, you will be more convincing and believable to people regardless of if they know you personally or not.

Chapter 8: Medical Treatments and Psychotherapy

In this chapter, we will be studying the different medical treatments and psychotherapy that are used to treat mental disorders like social anxiety. We will be taking a look at medical treatments like SSRIs and SNRIs, psychotherapy treatments like CBT, and other alternative therapy types like hypnosis and yoga. Let's dive right in.

Medical Treatments

When it comes to medical treatment for mental disorders like anxiety and depression, it is the most advertised form of treatment, but it doesn't necessarily mean that it is the most effective. Mental disorders like depression are about chemical imbalances in the brain, but it does not mean that it is only that. Medication often can help relieve the symptoms of moderate to severe depression but it does not solve the underlying problem and is not a long-term solution.

In order for you to make the right treatment decision for yourself, we will be exploring medication more in-depth in this subchapter. Antidepressants are a range of medications that are used to treat depression or other mental disorders. They are the most commonly prescribed medications these days. Antidepressants include SSRIs (serotonin reuptake inhibitors), SNRIs (serotonin-norepinephrine reuptake inhibitors, TCAs (tricyclic antidepressants), atypical antidepressants, and MAOIs (monoamine oxidase inhibitors).

Antidepressants are designed to adjust the neurotransmitters in the brain to help correct the balance of chemicals. When a person is in the trenches of suffering from the pain and anguish of depression, simply taking a pill can sound like a convenient and simple method of relief. However, it is important to keep in mind that depression isn't only caused by the imbalance of brain chemicals. Instead, it is a combination of that and other psychological, biological, and social factors that include coping skills, relationships, and lifestyle, all of which medication would not be able to address. However, this doesn't mean that antidepressants don't work.

When a person's depression is on a severe level, medication can be very helpful and even lifesaving. Although it can help relieve symptoms for some people, antidepressants do not cure depression and is not a recommended long-term solution. As more time passes, people who initially found antidepressants to be useful can slip back into depression. This goes the same for the people who stop taking the medication. In addition, antidepressants also come with undesirable side effects, so it is important for people to consider the pros and cons when they are considering taking depression medication.

People who have mild to moderate depression find that exercise, self-help strategies, and therapy works just as well, or even better than medication. It also doesn't come with any side effects. Like we mentioned earlier in this chapter, even if you decide to take antidepressants, it is also important to pursue other changes in your life so that you can address whatever the underlying issue may be and to overcome depression for good.

Let's learn a little bit more about the different types of antidepressants and what their side effects are:

SSRIs

This is the most commonly prescribed type of antidepressant that is from the SSRI class of medications. This includes drugs like Zoloft, Prozac, and Paxil. SSRIs function on serotonin (a neurotransmitter) which is a chemical in the brain that is responsible for regulating moods.

SNRIs

Just like the name suggests, SNRIs stand for serotonin and norepinephrine reuptake inhibitors. These drugs act on serotonin and norepinephrine. Drugs that have this include Effexor, Pristiq, Cymbalta, and Fetzima. These drugs can be used to treat depression, anxiety, and pain.

Side Effects of SSRIs and SNRIs

Since these neurotransmitters play a huge part in a person's mental clarity, digestion, sleep, and pain, SSRIs and SNRIs cause a wide range of unpleasant side effects. They include:

- Headaches
- Constipation
- Diarrhea
- Dry mouth
- Fatigue or sleepiness
- Excessive sweating
- Tremors
- Weight gain
- Dizziness
- Decreased sex drive
- Restlessness
- Anxiety
- Insomnia
- Nausea

Atypical Antidepressants

Atypical antidepressants mean that they don't fit into the other classes of antidepressants, and they target different neurotransmitters in a person's brain to regulate mood and change brain chemistry. These drugs include Trintellix, Vilibryd, Serzone, Desyrel, Remeron, and Wellbutrin. The side effects differ depending on which specific drug the person takes, but many atypical antidepressants caused blurred vision, dry mouth, nervousness, sleepiness, weight gain, fatigue and nausea.

MAOIs

Monoamine oxidase inhibitors (MAOIs) were the first antidepressants to have been developed. They are an effective drug but have mostly been replaced by newer antidepressants like SSRIs and SNRIs as they are both safe and have fewer side effects. MAOIs usually requires the patient to have dietary restrictions, such as avoiding any other types of medications. The main side effect of MAOIs is that they can cause high blood pressure if it's taken with certain medications or food.

Beta-Blockers

Beta-blockers are medications that help to reduce a person's blood pressure. They work by blocking the hormone epinephrine. Beta-blockers cause a person's heart to beat slower and with lower force, which lowers their blood pressure. They also help to open up a person's arteries and veins to help with blood flow.

Benzodiazepines

Benzodiazepines are a type of drug that is used to treat those with anxiety, depression, alcohol withdrawal, and sleep disorders. They work by initiating a tranquilizing chemical in a person's brain to help them feel more calm and relaxed. Side effects include feelings of depression, drowsiness, dizziness, and poor coordination. In addition, mixing alcohol with benzodiazepines can be fatal. These drugs are also highly addictive and are not normally prescribed unless a person is showing severe symptoms of anxiety and depression.

Hypnosis

Most of us know hypnosis as what we've seen in movies and TV shows. Contrary to common belief, hypnosis is a lot more than just traveling into a trancelike state after using some airy-fairy technique. Hypnotherapy is a process where the therapist helps you relax and focus. The state they try to lead you into is similar to sleep, but your mind will be focused and more open to suggestions.

When a person is in this relaxed state, hypnotherapists believe that it is easier to focus your subconscious mind. This allows people to take a deeper look at some of their inner-issues. Hypnotherapy is used to help with the following:

- Help relax and rewire a person's anxious mind
- Instilling healthier habits (e.g., helping with weight loss)

- Exploring repressed memories

Hypnotherapy is usually used as a complementary treatment with Cognitive Behavioral Therapy. Due to the relaxed state that you're put in, it is easy to prevent symptoms of anxiety that people may feel.

Cognitive Behavioral Therapy (CBT)

Cognitive Behavioral Therapy works by emphasizing the relationship between our thoughts, feelings, and behaviors. When you begin to change any of these components, you start to initiate change in the others. The goal of CBT is to help lower the amount of worry you do and increase the overall quality of your life. Here are the 8 basic principles of how Cognitive Behavioral Therapy works:

1. <u>CBT will help provide a new perspective of understanding your problems</u>.

A lot of times, when an individual has been living with a problem for a long time in their life, they may have developed unique ways of understanding it and dealing with it. Usually, this just maintains the problem or makes it worse. CBT is effective in helping you look at your problem from a new perspective, and this will help you learn other ways of understanding your problem and learning a new way of dealing with it.

2. <u>CBT will help you generate new skills to work out your problem</u>.

You probably know that understanding a problem is one matter, and dealing with it is entirely another can of worms. To help start changing your problem, you will need to develop new skills that will help you change your thoughts, behaviors, and emotions that are affecting your anxiety and mental health. For instance, CBT will help you achieve new ideas about your problem and begin to use and test them in your daily life. Therefore, you will be more capable of making up your own mind regarding the root issue that is causing these negative symptoms.

3. <u>CBT relies on teamwork and collaboration</u>
    <u>between the client and therapist (or</u>
    <u>program)</u>.

CBT will require you to be actively involved in
the entire process, and your thoughts and ideas
are extremely valuable right from the beginning
of the therapy. You are the expert when it comes
to your thoughts and problems. The therapist is
the expert when it comes to acknowledging the
emotional issues. By working as a team, you will
be able to identify your problems and have your
therapist better address them. Historically, the
more the therapy advances, the more the client
takes the lead in finding techniques to deal with
the symptoms.

4. <u>The goal of CBT is to help the client become</u>
    <u>their own therapist</u>.

Therapy is expensive; we all know that. One of
the goals of CBT is to not have you become
overly dependent on your therapist because it is
not feasible to have therapy forever. When
therapy comes to an end and you do not become

your own therapist, you will be at high risk for a relapse.

However, if you are able to become your own therapist, you will be in a good spot to face the hurdles that life throws at you. In addition, it is proven that having confidence in your own ability to face hardship is one of the best predictors of maintaining the valuable information you got from therapy. By playing an active role during your sessions, you will be able to gain the confidence needed to face your problems when the sessions are over.

5. <u>CBT is succinct and time-limited</u>.

As a rule of thumb, CBT therapy sessions typically last over the course of 10 to 20 sessions. Statistically, when therapy goes on for many months, there is a higher risk of the client becoming dependent on the therapist. Once you have gained a new perspective and understanding of your problem, and are equipped with the right skills, you are able to use them to solve future problems. It is crucial in

CBT for you to try out your new skills in the real world. By actually dealing with your own problem hands-on without the security of recurring therapy sessions, you will be able to build confidence in your ability to become your own therapist.

6. <u>CBT is direction based and structured.</u>

CBT typically relies on a fundamental strategy called 'guided recovery.' By setting up some experiments with your therapist, you will be able to experiment with new ideas to see if they reflect your reality accurately. In other words, your therapist is your guide while you are making discoveries in CBT. The therapist will not tell you whether you are right or wrong but instead, they will help develop ideas and experiments to help you test these ideas.

7. <u>CBT is based on the present, "here and now".</u>

Although we know that our childhood and developmental history play a big role in who we are today, one of the principles of CBT actually distinguishes between what caused the problem and what is maintaining the problem presently. In a lot of cases, the reasons that maintain a problem are different than the ones that originally caused it.

For example, if you fall off while riding a horse, you may become afraid of horses. Your fear will continue to be maintained if you begin to start avoiding all horses and refuse to ride one again. In this example, the fear was called by the fall, but by avoiding your fear, you are continuing to maintain it. Unfortunately, you cannot change the fact that you had fallen off the horse but you can change your behaviors when it comes to avoidance. CBT primarily focuses on the factors that are maintaining the problem because these factors are susceptible to change.

8. <u>Worksheet exercises are significant elements of CBT therapy</u>.

Unfortunately, reading about CBT or going to one session of therapy a week is not enough to change our ingrained patterns of thinking and behaving. During CBT, the client is always encouraged to apply their new skills into their daily lives. Although most people find CBT therapy sessions to be very intriguing, it does not lead to change in reality if you do not exercise the skills you have learned.

These eight principles will be your guiding light throughout your Cognitive Behavioral Therapy. By learning, understanding, and applying these eight principles, you will be in a good position to invest your time and energy into becoming your own therapist and achieving your personal goals.

Based on research, individuals who are highly motivated to try exercises outside of sessions tend to find more value in therapy than those who don't. Keep in mind that other external factors still have an effect on your success, but your motivation is one of the most significant factors. By following CBT using the principles above, you should be able to remain highly motivated throughout CBT.

Challenging Your Unhelpful Thinking Styles

Once you are able to identify your own unhelpful thinking styles, you can begin trying to reshape those thoughts into something more realistic and factual. We learned about unhelpful thinking styles in a previous chapter. Here, we will be learning how to challenge these thoughts in order to build a healthier thinking style.

Keep in mind that it takes a lot of effort and dedication to change our own thoughts, so don't get frustrated if you are not succeeding right away. You probably have had these thoughts for a while, so don't expect it to change overnight.

Probability Overestimation

If you find that you have thoughts about a possible negative outcome, but you are noticing that you often overestimate the probability, try asking yourself the questions below to re-evaluate your thoughts.

- Based on my experience, what is the probability that this thought will come true realistically?
- What are the other possible results from this situation? Is the outcome that I am thinking of now the only possible one? Does my feared outcome have the highest probability out of the other outcomes?
- Have I ever experienced this type of situation before? If so, what happened? What have I learned from these past experiences that would be helpful to me now?
- If a friend or loved one is having these thoughts, what would I say to them?

Catastrophizing

- If the prediction that I am afraid of really did come true, how bad would it really be?
- If I am feeling embarrassed, how long will this last? How long will other people remember/talk about it? What are all the different things they could be saying? Is it 100% that they will only think bad things?

- I am feeling uncomfortable right now, but is this really a horrible or unbearable outcome?
- What are the other alternatives for how this situation could turn out?
- If a friend or loved one was having these thoughts, what would I say to them?

Mind Reading

- Is it possible that I really know what other people's thoughts are? What are the other things they could be thinking about?
- Do I have any evidence to support my own assumptions?
- In the scenario that my assumption is true, what is so bad about it?

Personalization

- What other elements might be playing a role in the situation? Could it be the other person's stress, deadlines, or mood?
- Does somebody always have to be at blame?
- A conversation is never just one person's responsibility.

- Were any of these circumstances out of my control?

Should Statements

- Would I be holding the same standards to a loved one or a friend?
- Are there any exceptions?
- Will someone else do this differently?

All or Nothing Thinking

- Is there a middle ground or grey area that I am not considering?
- Would I judge a friend or loved one in the same way?
- Was the entire situation 100% negative? Was there any part of the situation that I handled well?
- Is having/showing some anxiety such a horrible thing?

Selective Attention/Memory

- What are the positive elements of the situation? Am I ignoring those?

- Would a different person see this situation differently?

- What strengths do I have? Am I ignoring those?

Negative Core Beliefs

- Do I have any evidence that supports my negative beliefs?

- Is this thought true in every situation?

- Would a loved one or friend agree with my self-belief?

Once you catch yourself using these unhelpful thinking patterns, ask yourself the above questions to begin changing your own thoughts. Remember, the core basis of CBT is the idea that your own thoughts affect your emotions which then influences your behavior. By catching and changing your thoughts before it spirals, you will be in control of your emotions and behavior as well.

Other Types of Therapy

Before Cognitive Behavioral Therapy was developed, there were more traditional methods of psychotherapy. This type of therapy is more reflective of the therapy that we usually see in the media. Usually, traditional forms of speaking therapy include a lot of discussion about one's past and how their upbringing may be influencing their emotions and behaviors in the present day. We will be taking a look at two types of speaking therapies; Psychodynamic therapy and acceptance and commitment therapy.

Psychodynamic Therapy

Psychodynamic therapy is similar to psychoanalytic therapy in a way that is an in-depth form of talking therapy based on psychoanalysis principles and theories. However, psychodynamic therapy is not as focused on the relationship between the client and therapist but is more focused on the client's relationship with their external world. Usually, psychodynamic therapy is not as long as psychoanalytic therapy when it comes to the number of sessions and frequency; however, this differs case by case.

Psychodynamic therapy is mainly used to treat depression and other severe psychological disorders. It focuses especially on the people who may have lost meaning in their lives and struggle with maintaining and forming personal relationships. Studies have found that people who suffer from eating disorders, addiction, and social anxiety disorders benefit from psychodynamic therapy. During psychodynamic therapy, the client is encouraged to speak about anything that comes to mind including dreams, desires, fantasies, current issues, through the help of the therapist.

The goal of this therapy is for the client to experience a reduction of their depression systems but also achieve other benefits such as better use of their own abilities and talents, increasing self-esteem and an improved ability to develop and maintain better relationships. The client may continue to experience the benefits even after this therapy has ended. Some patients may find that short-term therapy (less than one year) is sufficient; some other patients may require long-term therapy in order to gain lasting effects.

Psychodynamic therapy's theories and techniques distinguish itself from other forms of therapy by focusing on acknowledging, recognizing, expressing, understanding, and overcoming contradictory and negative feelings and repressed emotions in order to help the client improve their interpersonal relationships and experiences. This includes helping the client understand how their previous repressed emotions affect their current behavior, relationships, and decision-making.

This type of therapy also aims to help the client who may be aware of their social difficulties but doesn't have the tools or skills to overcome this problem by themselves. During this therapy, the clients will learn to analyze and resolve their current issues and then change their behavior in their current relationships through the use of deep exploration and analysis of their past experiences and emotions.

Acceptance and Commitment Therapy

Acceptance and commitment therapy (ACT) is a therapy strategy that uses mindfulness and acceptance strategies in conjunction with behavior and commitment strategies. Together, these two strategies are used to increase a person's psychological flexibility. The definition of psychological flexibility, in this case, is the ability to be in touch with the present moment and based on what situation is perceived, being able to change your behavior.

The main objective of ACT is not to get rid of all negative and difficult feelings. Instead, it is to practice being present in the moment and to pay attention to what life is bringing in the present moment. ACT helps people open themselves up to unpleasant feelings and to help them learn to not overreact to them.

Alternative Treatments

There are numerous alternative treatments that one can employ to help with their anxiety or depression. The most popular alternative treatments present-day are yoga and taking dietary supplements. Let's take a look at each.

Yoga

Yoga is a type of exercise that has become increasingly popular over the years. Originally, the purpose of yoga was to allow the person practicing it to become more in touch with their mind and body. Depending on which type of yoga you are interested in trying, some types are more focused on the mental exercise rather than the physical. Yoga is actually a form of mindfulness, as we learned about earlier in this book. It encourages a person to focus on what is happening at the moment and practicing to focus on the present rather than allowing your thoughts to wander off.

Many people have found success in Yoga as a cure to their anxiety. On top of helping you increase your mindfulness, Yoga offers good exercise which helps regulate the brain chemicals that are responsible for feelings of happiness and contentedness.

Dietary Supplements

Based on research done by the Anxiety and Depression Association of America, various supplements such as omega-3, vitamins, and herbal remedies can help relieve symptoms of anxiety. There are numerous herbal remedies that do not have enough research to support their effectiveness and safety. If you are interested in trying out different dietary supplements, I advise you to test the ones that have been backed up by research.

Let's take a look at a few dietary supplements that have been proven to help with anxiety symptoms:

- **Vitamin D:**Vitamin D plays an important role in a person's mood regulation and brain health. There are not many foods that contain vitamin D, so often, people are deficient in vitamin D. Spending time in the sunlight also gives your body more Vitamin D and improves the absorption of it.

- **Vitamin B complex:** A research study in 2017 found that people who had low levels of vitamin B-12 were more likely to have anxiety or depression.

- **Magnesium:** A small study in 2016 found that people who were diagnosed with anxiety benefited from taking magnesium supplements every day.

- **L-theanine:** L-theanine is an amino acid that can be found in black and green tea. Research has found evidence that it can act as a mild anti-anxiety and mild-sedative agent.

- **Multivitamin and mineral supplements:** A supplement that contains a wide range of minerals and vitamins can help those with depression and/or anxiety. A very recent study in 2019 found that supplements that contained; B vitamins, C vitamins, zinc, calcium, and magnesium significantly decreased anxiety levels in young adults and adolescents.

- **Valerian root:** The valerian plant has been used as medicine by people for thousands of years. The NCCIH stated that the valerian root is safe for consumption over short periods. However, there is not any research that indicates that it is safe for long-term consumption.

Conclusion

Learning about your own anxiety and where it may be coming from is never an easy task. In fact, it is one that is taxing and emotionally exhausting. However, strong knowledge regarding your own anxiety and knowing what your triggers are is an important first step to healing from it. It is important to find the right treatment for your anxiety; however, what's more important is understanding what anxiety is and recognizing its symptoms and causes.

Throughout this book, you learned about numerous treatments that can help manage your anxiety. You learned about self-help coping methods, such as social coping and emotional coping. Through these methods, you can learn to use simple skills that you already have by improving upon them.

You also learned about breathing exercises and reducing negative thinking to help with your everyday mental state. In addition, you learned about numerous lifestyle changes you can make to lessen anxiety. This paired with official treatment methods like psychotherapy and medication can help you reduce your anxiety significantly.

The next step in your journey is to try numerous methods and figure out which ones work best for you. Although medication may have worked for a friend that has anxiety, it doesn't necessarily mean it will work for you. Most treatment methods, including medication, take up to six weeks for the person to experience the benefits so don't give up on your treatment plan quickly. Stick with it for 6 – 8 weeks to properly test out its effectiveness on yourself.

Remember, practice is a huge component in recovering from social anxiety. Whether it's CBT methods that you're practicing or if you're simply trying to get back out in society, keep practicing and making small steps: I promise you that they will all add up.

The last takeaway that I want to pass on to you is to try multiple treatments. This is the best way for you to receive benefits the quickest and most effectively. Try to pair up your treatment method of choice with something else.

For instance, if your doctor has recommended CBT as your choice of therapy, try to pair it up with a lifestyle change or meditation. Trying more than one treatment method at once will increase your chances of finding your optimum treatment plan. Stick with it and don't give up. It is in your power to beat your anxiety.

Final words:

Here we are... ;-)

"Overcome Social Anxiety" is over.

Thank you again for having read this book.

I hope that reading it has been useful to you, that it may have served you to know yourself better and improve your life!

If you prefer to use the digital version to help you organize an action plan:

https://www.amazon.com/dp/B0825WYM5Q

If you prefer to use the audiobook version, it will be available soon.

I wish you the very best of luck with the achievement of your goals!!

Did you enjoy this guide?

If you enjoyed this book, it would be awesome if you could leave a quick review on Amazon. Your feedback is much appreciated and I would love to hear from you.

Leave a Review on Amazon

Thanks so much!!

More books by Dalton McKay:

Self-Esteem Workbook: A Practical Guide to Help You Overcome Self-Doubt and Insecurity, Gain Better Confidence, and Find Your Inner Strength. Discover Your Hidden Potential and Change Your Life in 30 Days. (Link)

More books by Dalton McKay:

Effective Communication Skills: How to Talk to Anyone. A Practical Guide to Boost Your Conversation and Writing Skills in the Workplace, Improve Charisma and Build Healthy Interpersonal Relationships (Link)

More books by Dalton McKay:

**Self-Discipline Mastery
A Practical Guide to Improve YOUR Self
Control, Overcome Failures, Develop
Mental Toughness. Learn How to
Successfully Achieve YOUR Long-Term
Goals the Easy Way. (Link)**

CPSIA information can be obtained
at www.ICGtesting.com
Printed in the USA
LVHW051439201120
672130LV00008B/360